C0-CCO-949

From the library of
Dean Robert J. Trebar

Much loved, sorely missed

The universe is made from silence.

"*The universe is made from silence.*"

(QUOTATION PHOTOGRAPHED FROM VISITORS BOOK AT A MILITARY CEMETERY IN FRANCE)

TEARS *of* STONE

WORLD WAR I REMEMBERED

TRÄNEN *aus* STEIN

ERINNERUNGEN AN DEN ERSTEN WELTKRIEG

LARMES de PIERRE

COMMÉMORATION DE LA GRANDE GUERRE

Jane Alden Stevens

For GORDON, CONNOR *and* ZOE
the lights of my life

&

For MY PARENTS
who encouraged me to be curious

&

For ANDREW
without whom this project would have been a shadow of itself

Für GORDON, CONNOR *und* ZOE
die Lichter in meinem Leben

&

Für MEINE ELTERN
die mir Mut machten, neugierig zu sein

&

Für ANDREW
ohne den dieses Projekt nur ein Schatten seiner selbst gewesen wäre

À GORDON, CONNOR *et* ZOE
les lumières de ma vie

&

À MES PARENTS
qui ont éveillé mon esprit de curiosité

&

À ANDREW
sans qui ce projet n'aurait été que l'ombre de lui-même

Catalogue copyright 2004 Jane Alden Stevens

All rights reserved. No part of this book may be reproduced in any form or by any electronic or
mechanical means, including information storage and retrieval systems, without
permission in writing from the author, except by a reviewer, who may quote brief passages in a review.

Alle Rechte vorbehalten. Bilder oder Text aus diesem Band dürfen ohne ausdrückliche
schriftliche Genehmigung des Autors in keiner Form reproduziert oder übersetzt werden.

*Tous droits réservés. Il est interdit de reproduire ou traduire toute image ou tout
texte de ce volume, sous quelque forme que ce soit, sans l'autorisation expresse écrite de l'auteur.*

Web site: www.janealdenstevens.com
E-mail: contact@janealdenstevens.com

This catalogue was edited by Ann H. Stevens, East River Editorial, Rochester, NY

Design and production by Bill Buckett, Rochester, NY, and Jennifer Wolfe, Rochester, NY

Tritone separations by Thomas Palmer, Newport, RI

Printing by Meridian Printing, East Greenwich, RI

ISBN: 0-9743338-0-8 (softbound) | ISBN: 0-9743338-1-6 (casebound)

The author gratefully acknowledges the generous funding of
the following organizations in support of this project:

Die Autorin dankt den folgenden Organisationen für
ihre großzügige Unterstützung bei diesem Projekt:

*L'auteur exprime ses remerciements et sa reconnaissance aux organisations
suivantes pour leur généreux soutien dans le cadre de ce projet:*

THE OHIO ARTS COUNCIL

THE UNIVERSITY OF CINCINNATI

THE ENGLISH-SPEAKING UNION

TEARS *of* STONE

WORLD WAR I REMEMBERED

Photographs by

JANE ALDEN STEVENS

Foreword by

DONOVAN WEBSTER

TRÄNEN *aus* STEIN

ERINNERUNGEN AN DEN ERSTEN WELTKRIEG

Fotografien von

JANE ALDEN STEVENS

Vorwort von

DONOVAN WEBSTER

LARMES *de* PIERRE

COMMÉMORATION DE LA GRANDE GUERRE

Photographies de

JANE ALDEN STEVENS

Avant-propos de

DONOVAN WEBSTER

CINCINNATI, OHIO, USA

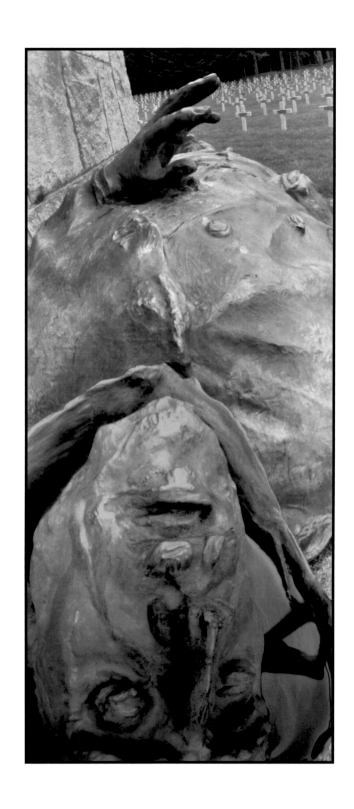

LE WETTSTEIN, FRENCH MILITARY CEMETERY, FRANCE

Französischer Militärfriedhof Le Wettstein, Frankreich | *Le Wettstein, Cimetière militaire français, France*

CONTENTS   INHALT   *SOMMAIRE*

We came to see Uncle, Great Uncle, Great Great Uncle's Grave. He lives through us.

We came to see uncle Great Uncle Great Great Uncle Grave. He lives through us.

"*We came to see Uncle, Great Uncle, Great Great Uncle's Grave. He lives through us.*"

(QUOTATION PHOTOGRAPHED FROM VISITORS BOOK AT A MILITARY CEMETERY IN FRANCE)

FOREWORD   VORWORT   *AVANT-PROPOS*

THE UNSETTLING VISION *of* JANE ALDEN STEVENS

by DONOVAN WEBSTER

*D*ON'T KID YOURSELF. ON THIS EARTH, especially after more than 100 million people have died at another's hand in 20th-century wars alone, haunted places are everywhere.

Their names are a shadow-draped litany: Omaha Beach, Choeung Ek, Inchon, Hamburger Hill, Stalingrad, Kigali, Kuwait City, Khe Sanh, The Moro Lands of the southern Philippines, Auschwitz, Luanda, Nanking, Hiroshima…the list goes on and on.

And those are just a few examples from our most recent century. Obviously, this group of hallowed grounds doesn't include the thundering, head-lopping crusades of Ghengis Khan across Asia or the Greeks' slaughter of the Persians at Marathon. It doesn't take into account Agincourt, Waterloo, or Emperor Napoleon's slow bleed (and subsequent retreat) in 1812, where his 422,000-man Grand Army invaded Moscow as it was burned to the ground, then limped home through the snow to Paris with fewer than 10,000 men still alive at journey's end. The list of 20th-century haunted lands doesn't make note of the mayhem at Troy or the killing fields around Tennessee's Shiloh Meeting House, where in April of 1862 more than 24,000 men died or went missing in two short days. At Shiloh, area creeks were said to have run pink with blood for days.

Show up at any of these places on a foggy autumn dawn and you'll sense the lingering chaos and death as surely as you can feel the breeze against your cheek. Before you know it, the havoc that once littered these now-peaceful landscapes is on your shoes and inside your lungs. It's inescapable. And at places like these, it's everywhere.

Few people understand this haunted sense as well as Jane Alden Stevens, a fact made eloquently clear through the book you're now holding in your hands.

During five trips to World War I battlegrounds and memorials—in France, Belgium, England, Germany, and the Alsace-Lorraine—over a span of nearly two years, Stevens visited perhaps the 20th century's most haunted places: the European plains and hillsides where World War I's preponderance of battles were fought. And as she traveled to these places, in her mind she carried one simple—yet endlessly complex—objective. Somehow, Stevens intended to visually capture their off-kilter character through the simplicity of horizontally framed, black-and-white photographs.

The result is stunningly remarkable: personal yet universal, profoundly respectful but inherently pacifist. The images work both singly and in the aggregate. Employing extraordinary visual elegance and restraint, Stevens has managed to bring alive the spooky reverence of these battlegrounds—not an easy trick when using a language that has no words, and whose result—by its very nature—lies passively on paper.

Still, if there are exceptionally haunted landscapes on earth, the sites of the great sieges of World War I—especially at Ypres, Belgium, and at Verdun in east-central France—certainly rank among the richest. Their horrors were the opening of a modern bank where mechanized death became coin of the realm, and that coin was squandered with epic disconcern.

At Ypres, Belgium, on April 22, 1915, after a ten-month standoff along a barely wavering battle line, the morning arrived with a non-stop German barrage of artillery not yet seen on the war's Western Front. Everywhere across Ypres and its outlying countryside, huge geysers of black mud spewed into the air as explosions from the Germans' celebrated 17-inch howitzers—whose shells weighed more than a ton each—began tearing gargantuan hunks of earth from the Allied trenches. Then, as the day-long artillery blasts finally began to wane with the day's tilt toward evening, a dense and greenish-yellow mist began to rise from German trenches to the northeast. The heavy cloud hung near the ground, then began blowing downwind toward the forward Allied forces and Ypres beyond. It was the war's first wave of chlorine gas.

The French troops were the first to feel it, and—coughing and gasping—those who could climb from their trenches fled in the sunset. Many others died by drowning, their lungs filling with liquid as millions of tiny air sacs inside them were burst by noxious poison. Then the British nearby began to retch from it, too. And from behind the rolling cloud, the German troops—leery of the effects of chlorine—advanced cautiously as the gas carried further to the southwest. Amazingly, the Kaiser's Army stopped 2,500 yards short of the city, though they could have easily taken Ypres that evening. By the following morning, as the fight for Ypres began anew, fresh rounds of gas asphyxiants—including mustard gas and phosgene—also began flowing to the front from both sides.

The polite rules of 19th-century war were now forgotten, and any weapon man could conjure was on the table to be used. The automated meat grinder that became World War I's trench warfare could now begin mowing down men in far greater handfuls. Before the engagement for Ypres was over, the British would lose 60,000 men, the French 10,000, and the Germans some 35,000.

But the losses at Ypres were nothing compared with those soon to follow at Verdun, France. On the beautiful, snow-bright morning of February 21, 1916—at 7:15 AM and after an eight-month buildup—German artillery of every order began to fall on the French fortresses and trenches encircling the city. And for the next ten hours, the shells continued to rain down as the entrenched Frenchmen—crouched over and praying—waited for the onslaught to end.

By noon of that first day, no habitable structures were left in any of the nine villages outlying Verdun, and the heat from the hundreds of thousands—possibly millions—of artillery explosions had melted the layer of snow that, only hours earlier, coated the countryside's fields and rooftops. The result was a world of frigid, bomb-cratered, ice-rimed mud.

Then came the siege's truly terrifying part. Just before sunset, as the barrage finally ended, the Germans started their advance. And in the trenches around Verdun, as a tide of re-freezing snowmelt began to lift around the Frenchmen's shins, those defenders of Verdun not killed by explosions or fragmentation shells readied to defend their city. The landscape between them and their aggressors was shredded. Artillery explosions had denuded whole forests, leaving them as smoldering pickets of tree trunks, the vegetation itself having been blown to pieces. In place of the trees were now explosion pocks and slick mud.

But the Germans had still another horror up their sleeves. To make sure the battlefield was completely cleared of obstacles during this most violent of sunsets, they chose to scour away the remaining brush and downed trees by debuting their newest invention: the flame-thrower.

As the fire-breathing throng began its advance, the Frenchmen steadied their rifles among the clods of dirt fronting their trenches and began to defend themselves. Soon, the French learned that if they shot the fuel tank each flame-thrower carried on his back, the tanks would explode. Hundreds of German infantrymen were immolated; the others kept coming. In another hour, the Germans were at the trenches, and the two armies began to maul one another with whatever tools they could find: knives and fists, rocks and rifle butts.

In the hills above Verdun, that kind of fighting continued every day for ten months; then it sputtered and sparked for 18 more. And all to contest a line of battle that had shifted back and forth only a few miles by the war's end. When the siege for Verdun was finally over, better than 1,000,000 soldiers had been devoured by the fighting. And in what may be the most grisly war statistic ever, only 290,000 bodies were ever recovered—with only 160,000 of these dead ever being identified. The rest were simply removed from the battlefield as parts.

In the end, the majority of Verdun's million fallen men—more than 710,000 troops (enough adult males to populate a major city)—were simply written off as lost, swallowed by the war's explosions and mud. The new, mechanical, manufacturing-driven world of 20th-century war had destroyed them completely. In the heartless bookkeeping of modern war, the whole group was merely zeroed out.

These kinds of tragedies can stain landscapes forever.

For Jane Alden Stevens, the desire to render the First World War's losses through oblique, glancing images was the challenge. And she has succeeded astonishingly in meeting it.

No one can look at the image of water draining down the marble steps at Britain's Chatham Naval Memorial *(Plate No. 26)* and not imagine, for a moment, that this dark runoff is blood. In the landscape photos, it is impossible not to notice that, almost 90 years after the war's end, the earth is still rumpled and disfigured by bomb craters. Consider the small, artillery-blasted area near Hill 62 in Ypres (just two mounds of earth distant from the war's first use of poison gas)*(Plate No. 14)*. Trees have once again grown up to shade the soil, but the evidence of 1915's horrible spring of shelling is unmistakable. Old trenches run to an equally aged fortification, and the shine of muddy water on the trench's floor evokes an April of cold rain—where choking gas and exploding artillery were everywhere. You can almost feel bullets slashing the air above the trench's outworks.

In Stevens' photo from atop Verdun's tragic Fort Douaumont *(Plate No. 1)*—whose tired-looking gray concrete walls fell to the Germans five days after the siege began, becoming a tomb for 679 Germans who died in a single munitions accident deep inside—a tangle of 1916-vintage concertina wire dominates. The nest of rusting steel strands seems to say: Yes, these losses are remembered; this place is revered. But, hauntingly, modern humans are absent from the photo.

"One of the things I wanted to do with this project," Stevens says, "was to explore the persistence of human memory. Do we actively remember the losses of wars from well before our time?

How important do the memorials we build in the aftermath of war remain after the passage of time? And how does the land itself remind us of our violent past?"

Are there haunted landscapes on earth? You bet. Just turn the page.

DONOVAN WEBSTER

AUTHOR, *AFTERMATH: THE REMNANTS OF WAR*

DIE UNSTILLBARE VISION *der* JANE ALDEN STEVENS

von DONOVAN WEBSTER

MACHEN SIE SICH NICHTS VOR. AUF DIESER ERDE, insbesondere nachdem mehr als 100 Millionen Menschen alleine in den Kriegen des 20. Jahrhunderts durch die Hand eines anderen starben, gibt es überall geschundene Orte.

Ihre Namen sind eine schattenverhangene Litanei: Omaha Beach, Choeung Ek, Inchon, Hamburger Hill, Stalingrad, Kigali, Kuwait City, Khe Sanh, das Land der Moro auf den südlichen Philippinen, Auschwitz, Luanda, Nanking, Hiroshima… Die Liste nimmt kein Ende.

Dies sind nur einige Beispiele aus dem jüngsten Jahrhundert. Offenbar beinhaltet diese Liste von geweihtem Boden nicht die donnernden, Köpfe abschlagenden Kreuzzüge von Dschingis Khan durch Asien oder das Gemetzel der Griechen an den Persern bei Marathon. Außen vor bleiben auch Azincourt, Waterloo oder das langsame Ausbluten von Kaiser Napoleon im Jahre 1812, als seine 422.000 Mann starke Große Armee in Moskau einfiel und es bis auf die Grundmauern niederbrannte. Und sein darauf folgender Rückzug: Von Moskau schleppte er sich durch den Schnee zurück nach Paris, weniger als 10.000 Mann waren am Ende der Reise noch am Leben. Die Liste der geschundenen Orte des 20. Jahrhunderts läßt das Massaker von Troja außer acht, genauso wie die Schlachtfelder um das Shiloh Meeting House in Tennessee, wo im April 1862 in nur zwei kurzen Tagen mehr als 24.000 Männer starben oder vermißt wurden. Man erzählt sich, daß die Bäche in Shiloh tagelang vom Blut rot gefärbt waren.

Fahren Sie an einem nebligen Herbstabend zu irgendeinem dieser Orte und Sie werden lauerndes Chaos und Tod genauso sicher spüren, wie Sie den Wind auf Ihren Wangen fühlen. Bevor Sie es merken, ist die Zerstörung, die einst diese nun friedlichen Landschaften heimsuchte, in Ihren Schuhen und in Ihrer Brust. Es gibt kein Entrinnen.

Wenige Menschen kennen dieses beklemmende Gefühl so gut wie Jane Alden Stevens. Das Buch in Ihren Händen macht dies deutlich.

Auf fünf Reisen zu Schlachtfeldern des Ersten Weltkriegs–in Frankreich, Belgien, Deutschland, in Elsaß-Lothringen–über einen Zeitraum von beinahe zwei Jahren besuchte Stevens die vielleicht am meisten geschundenen Orte des 20. Jahrhunderts: die europäischen Ebenen und Hügel, in denen die Mehrzahl der Schlachten des Ersten Weltkriegs geschlagen wurden. Und während sie zu diesen Orten reiste, hatte sie ein einfaches, wenn auch endlos komplexes, Ziel im Kopf. Stevens beabsichtigte, ihren ungeschönten Charakter durch die Einfachheit horizontal gerahmter Schwarz-Weiß-Fotografien visuell einzufangen.

Das Ergebnis ist beeindruckend und äußerst bemerkenswert: persönlich, universell, tiefgründig respektvoll, innerlich pazifistisch. Die Bilder wirken sowohl einzeln als auch in ihrer Gesamtheit. Unter Verwendung außergewöhnlicher visueller Eleganz und Beschränkung hat Jane Alden Stevens es geschafft, die Ehrerbietung für diese unheimlich wirkenden Schlachtfelder zum Leben zu erwecken–keine leichte Aufgabe, wenn man eine Sprache benutzt, die keine Worte kennt und deren Ergebnis–durch ihre ureigenste Natur–passiv auf Papier liegt.

Dennoch, wenn es besonders verwunschene Landschaften auf Erden gibt, zählen die Schauplätze der großen Belagerungen des Ersten Weltkriegs–insbesondere bei Ypern, Belgien, und bei Verdun im Osten Frankreichs–zu den ergiebigsten. Ihre Schrecken waren die Eröffnung einer modernen Bank, in welcher der mechanische Tod zur Währung des Königreiches wurde, und diese Währung wurde mit epischer Sorglosigkeit verschwendet.

In Ypern, Belgien, kam der Morgen des 22. April 1915. Der Kampf währte bereits zehn Monate entlang einer sich kaum bewegenden Frontlinie, mit einem ununterbrochenen deutschen Artilleriebeschuß, der an der Westfront bis dahin einmalig war. Überall in Ypern und auf dem umliegenden Land erhoben sich gewaltige Geysire aus schwarzem Schlamm in die Luft, als die Explosionen der gefeierten 17-Zoll-Haubitzen der Deutschen, deren Granaten jeweils mehr als eine Tonne wogen, damit begannen, riesige Stücke Erde aus den alliierten Schützengräben zu reißen. Als sich der Tag dem Abend zuneigte und die andauernden Explosionen nachließen, begann ein dichter und grünlich-gelber Nebel von den deutschen Schützengräben nach Nordosten aufzusteigen. Die schwere Wolke blieb nahe am Boden und begann dann, mit dem Wind auf die vorausliegenden alliierten Streitkräfte und nach Ypern zuzutreiben. So fing der erste Chlorgas-Angriff dieses Krieges an.

Die französischen Truppen bekamen es als erste zu spüren. Keuchend und nach Luft ringend flohen diejenigen, die aus ihren Schützengräben klettern konnten, in den Sonnenuntergang. Viele andere starben, sie ertranken, weil sich ihre Lungen mit Flüssigkeit füllten. Ihre Lungenbläschen wurden von dem tödlichen Gift zum Platzen gebracht. Auch die nahegelegenen Briten begannen zu leiden. Hinter der Wolke rückten die deutschen Truppen–selbst verunsichert von den Auswirkungen des Chlorgases–vorsichtig vor, während das Gas weiter nach Südwesten trieb. Überraschend stoppte die Armee des Kaisers 2.500 m vor der Stadt, obwohl sie an diesem Abend Ypern leicht hätte einnehmen können. Am folgenden Morgen, als der Kampf um Ypern erneut begann, wurden neue Giftgasattacken–auch Senfgas und Phosgen–von beiden Seiten der Front gestartet.

Die ehrenhaften Kriegsregeln des 19. Jahrhunderts waren nun vergessen, und jede Waffe, die der Mensch sich ausdenken konnte, kam hemmungslos zum Einsatz. Der automatische Fleischwolf, zu dem die Kriegsführung in den Schützengräben des Ersten Weltkriegs wurde, verarbeitete nun Menschen in viel größerer Menge. Bevor die Schlacht um Ypern vorbei war, verloren die Briten 60.000 Mann, die Franzosen 10.000 und die Deutschen etwa 35.000.

Aber die Verluste von Ypern waren nichts im Vergleich zu dem, was bald in Verdun, Frankreich, folgen sollte. An dem wunderschönen, schneeklaren Morgen des 21. Februar 1916–um 7:15 Uhr und nach einem acht Monate andauernden Aufmarsch–begann der deutsche Artilleriebeschuß auf die französischen Festungen und Schützengräben rund um die Stadt. Für die nächsten zehn Stunden regneten die Bomben nur so vom Himmel. Die festsitzenden Franzosen warteten geduckt und betend auf das Ende des Angriffs.

Am Mittag des ersten Tages waren in den neun Dörfern um Verdun keine bewohnbaren Gebäude mehr vorhanden, und die Hitze von hunderttausenden von Artillerieexplosionen–wahrscheinlich Millionen–hatte die Schneedecke schmelzen lassen, welche Stunden zuvor noch die Felder und Dächer der ländlichen Gegend bedeckte. Das Ergebnis war eine Welt aus eisigem Schlamm und Bombenkratern.

Dann kam der wirklich schreckliche Teil der Belagerung. Kurz vor Sonnenuntergang, als das Feuer endlich eingestellt war, begannen die Deutschen ihren Vormarsch. In den Schützengräben um Verdun, in denen die Flut geschmolzenen Schnees um die Schienbeine der Franzosen erneut gefror, machten sich die Überlebenden bereit, ihre Stadt zu verteidigen. Die Landschaft zwischen ihnen und ihren Angreifern war zerfetzt. Artillerieexplosionen hatten ganze Wälder kahlgeschlagen und nur rauchende Baumstümpfe übriggelassen. Die Vegetation selbst wurde in Stücke gerissen. Anstelle der Bäume waren dort nur noch Explosionspocken und glitschiger Schlamm.

Aber die Deutschen hielten noch weitere Schrecken bereit. Um sicherzustellen, daß das Schlachtfeld während dieses gewalttätigsten aller Sonnenuntergänge vollständig von Hindernissen befreit war, fegten sie die verbleibenden Büsche und umgestürzten Bäume beiseite, indem sie ihre neueste Erfindung zum Einsatz brachten: den Flammenwerfer.

Als die Feuer atmende Masse ihren Vormarsch begann, luden die Franzosen ihre Gewehre zwischen den Schmutzklumpen vor ihren Schützengräben und begannen, sich zu verteidigen. Bald schon fanden die Franzosen heraus, daß der Brennstofftank, den jeder Flammenwerfer auf dem Rücken trug, explodierte, wenn sie darauf schossen. Hunderte deutscher Infanteristen wurden geschlachtet; die anderen rückten nach. Eine Stunde später waren die Deutschen an den Schützengräben, und die beiden Armeen begannen, sich zu bekämpfen, mit allem, was sie finden konnten: Messer und Fäuste, Steine und Gewehrkolben.

Diese Art des Kampfes wurde in den Hügeln über Verdun jeden Tag fortgesetzt, zehn Monate lang; dann kam er ins Stocken, es folgten achtzehn weitere Monate. All dies nur wegen einer Frontlinie, die sich bis zum Ende des Krieges nur um wenige Meilen vorwärts oder rückwärts bewegte. Als die Belagerung von Verdun schließlich vorüber war, hatten die Kämpfe gut 1.000.000 Soldaten verschlungen. Die wohl grausigste Kriegsstatistik, die es jemals gab: nur 290.000 Körper wurden je geborgen–und nur 160.000 dieser Toten wurden je identifiziert. Der Rest wurde einfach in Stücken vom Schlachtfeld geschafft.

Am Ende wurden die meisten der Million gefallener Männer von Verdun–mehr als 710.000 Soldaten, genug erwachsene Männer, um eine Großstadt zu bevölkern–einfach als vermißt gemeldet, geschluckt von den Explosionen des Krieges und dem Schlamm. Die neue mechanische, durch Fabriken angetriebene Welt des Krieges des 20. Jahrhunderts hatte sie vollständig zerstört. In der herz-losen Buchführung der modernen Kriegsführung wurde die ganze Gruppe einfach nur abgeschrieben.

Diese Art von Tragödien können Landschaften für immer besudeln.

Für Jane Alden Stevens war es eine Herausforderung, die Verluste des Ersten Weltkriegs mit Hilfe von indirekten, flüchtigen Bildern wiederzugeben. Sie ist dieser Herausforderung erstaunlich gerecht geworden.

Niemand kann auf das Bild mit dem Wasser sehen, das die Marmorstufen der britischen Gedenkstätte für Seeleute in Chatham herabläuft *(Abbildung Nr. 26)*, ohne sich für einen Augenblick vorzustellen, daß das dunkle Rinnsal Blut ist. Die Landschaftsbilder zeigen deutlich, daß die Erde fast 90 Jahre nach Kriegsende noch durch Bombenkrater zerwühlt und entstellt ist. Nehmen Sie das kleine, von der Artillerie zerschossene Gebiet nahe dem Hügel 62 in Ypern (nur zwei Erdwälle vom ersten Giftgaseinsatz des Krieges entfernt) *(Abbildung Nr. 14)*. Es sind wieder Bäume gewachsen, um der Erdkrume ihren Schatten zu spenden, aber die Belege für den schrecklichen Bombenfrühling 1915 sind unverwechselbar. Alte Schützengräben laufen zu einer gleich alten Befestigung, und der Glanz von schlammigem Wasser auf dem Grund des Schützengrabens beschwört einen April mit kaltem Regen herauf–in dem atemraubendes Gas und explodierende Artillerie allgegenwärtig waren. Sie können beinahe die Geschosse fühlen, die durch die Luft über die Befestigungen der Schützengräben peitschten.

Auf Stevens' Bild von Verduns tragischem Fort Douaumont *(Abbildung Nr. 1)*, dessen müdewirkende grauen Betonwände fünf Tage nach Beginn der Belagerung an die Deutschen fielen und zum Grab für 679 Deutsche wurden, die bei einem einzigen Munitionsunfall im Inneren starben, dominiert ein Gewirr von Stacheldraht aus dem Jahre 1916. Das Nest aus rostenden Stahlsträngen scheint zu sagen: Ja, wir erinnern uns an die Verluste, dieser Ort wird verehrt. Aber es ist wie verhext, moderne Menschen fehlen auf dem Bild.

„Eines der Dinge, die ich mit diesem Projekt erreichen wollte", sagt Jane Alden Stevens, „war, die Dauerhaftigkeit des menschlichen Gedächtnisses zu erforschen. Erinnern wir uns aktiv an die Verluste von Kriegen weit vor unserer Zeit? Wie wichtig bleiben die Gedenkstätten, die wir in Nachkriegszeiten bauen, nachdem soviel Zeit vergangen ist? Und wie erinnert uns das Land selbst an unsere gewalttätige Vergangenheit?"

Gibt es geschundene Landschaften auf dieser Erde? Worauf Sie wetten können. Blättern Sie einmal um.

DONOVAN WEBSTER

AUTOR VON *AFTERMATH: THE REMNANTS OF WAR*

LA VISION TROUBLANTE *de* JANE ALDEN STEVENS

de DONOVAN WEBSTER

*I*L NE FAUT PAS SE FAIRE D'ILLUSIONS. SUR CETTE TERRE, *particulièrement après la mort de plus de 100 millions de personnes mortes par la main d'autrui pendant les guerres du XXe siècle seulement, on trouve partout des lieux hantés.*

Leurs noms sont comme une litanie drapée d'ombre: Omaha Beach, Choeung Ek, Inchon, Hamburger Hill, Stalingrad, Kigali, Koweït City, Khe Sanh, la terre des Moro aux Philippines du sud, Auschwitz, Luanda, Nankin, Hiroshima… la liste est longue.

Et ce ne sont là que quelques exemples de notre siècle le plus récent. Évidemment, ce groupe de lieux sacrés n'inclut pas les croisades retentissantes des coupeurs de têtes de Ghengis Khan en Asie, ou le massacre des Perses par les Grecs à Marathon. La liste ne tient pas compte d'Agincourt, de Waterloo ou de la sanglante campagne de l'Empereur Napoléon (suivie par sa retraite) en 1812, quand sa Grande Armée de 422.000 hommes envahit Moscou incendié, puis retourna tant bien que mal à Paris, dans la neige, avec moins de 10.000 hommes encore en vie à la fin du voyage. La liste des terres hantées du XXe siècle ne mentionne pas le chaos à Troie ni les champs meurtriers autour de Shiloh Meeting House au Tennessee, où en avril 1862, plus de 24.000 hommes sont morts ou ont été portés disparus en deux jours seulement. On dit qu'à Shiloh, les cours d'eau sont restés rouges de sang pendant des jours.

Visitez n'importe lequel de ces endroits par une brumeuse aube d'automne, et vous sentirez le chaos et la mort qui persistent, aussi sûrement que vous pourrez sentir la brise contre votre joue. Avant que vous ne le réalisiez, la désolation qui avait ravagé autrefois ces paysages, devenus maintenant paisibles, aura imprégné vos chaussures et pénétré dans vos poumons. C'est inéluctable. Et des endroits comme ceux-ci, il y en a partout.

Peu de gens comprennent ce sentiment de hantise aussi bien que Jane Alden Stevens, une évidence qu'elle traduit avec éloquence à travers ce livre maintenant entre vos mains.

Ayant effectué cinq voyages consacrés aux champs de bataille et mémoriaux de la Grande

Guerre–en France, en Belgique, en Angleterre, en Allemagne et en Alsace-Lorraine–durant près de deux ans, Stevens a visité les endroits peut-être les plus hantés du XXe siècle: les plaines et les coteaux européens où la plupart des batailles de la Première Guerre mondiale ont eu lieu. En se rendant dans ces endroits, elle a gardé à l'esprit un simple et seul objectif, bien qu'infiniment complexe. D'une manière ou d'une autre, l'intention de Stevens était de saisir visuellement leur caractère décalé à travers la simplicité de photographies en noir et blanc, cadrées horizontalement.

Le résultat est remarquable et éblouissant: personnel bien qu'universel, profondément respectueux bien que pacifiste en soi. Les images sont saisissantes, prises dans leur ensemble ou séparément. Stevens, avec une élégance et une sobriété extraordinaires, a réussi à faire revivre ces champs de bataille dans un hommage très émouvant–ce qui n'est pas une tâche facile lorsqu'on utilise un langage dépourvu de mots, et dont le résultat–de par sa nature même–repose sur du papier.

Cependant, s'il y a des paysages exceptionnellement hantés sur terre, les sites des grands sièges de la Première Guerre mondiale–particulièrement à Ypres, en Belgique et à Verdun, au centre-est de la France, sont certainement parmi les plus grands. Leurs horreurs ont fondé une banque moderne où la mort mécanisée est devenue une espèce sonnante et trébuchante, et cette monnaie a été dilapidée d'une manière épique et déconcertante.

À Ypres, en Belgique, le 22 avril 1915, après une impasse de dix mois le long d'une ligne de bataille à peine hésitante, le matin s'est annoncé par un barrage continu d'artillerie allemande jamais vu auparavant sur le Front occidental. Partout à Ypres et dans la campagne alentour, d'énormes geysers de boue noire accompagnaient les explosions des célèbres obusiers allemands de 17 pouces–dont les obus pesaient plus d'une tonne chacun–qui commençaient à arracher de gigantesques morceaux de terre des tranchées des Forces Alliées. Puis, alors que les détonations de l'artillerie qui avaient résonné toute la journée commençaient finalement à s'affaiblir à la tombée de la nuit, un brouillard dense de couleur verdâtre virant au jaune s'éleva peu à peu des tranchées allemandes au nord-est. Le gros nuage s'immobilisa à une faible hauteur du sol, puis commença à se déplacer dans la direction du vent, vers les Forces Alliées et en direction d'Ypres. C'était la première vague de gaz au chlore de la guerre.

Les troupes françaises furent les premières à le sentir; toussant et haletant, ceux qui pouvaient se hisser de leurs tranchées s'enfuirent avec la tombée de la nuit. Beaucoup d'autres moururent noyés, des millions de minuscules sacs d'air éclatant dans leurs poumons sous l'effet nocif du poison. Ensuite, les

Britanniques qui se trouvaient tout près commencèrent à leur tour à en souffrir. Et, derrière le nuage tournoyant, les troupes allemandes–tout en se méfiant des effets du chlore–avancèrent prudemment tandis que le gaz se déplaçait plus loin vers le sud-ouest. Chose surprenante, l'armée du Kaiser s'arrêta à 2.500 mètres de l'entrée de la ville, bien qu'elle eut pu facilement prendre Ypres ce soir-là. Le lendemain matin, alors que le combat pour Ypres reprenait, de nouvelles vagues de gaz asphyxiants, y compris du gaz moutarde et du phosgène–commencèrent à couler vers le front, de chaque côté.

Les règles polies de la guerre du XIXe siècle étaient à présent oubliées et toute arme conjurée par l'homme était en jeu, prête à être employée. Le hache-viande automatique qu'était devenue la guerre des tranchées de la Grande Guerre pouvait maintenant commencer à faucher des hommes en de bien plus grands nombres. Avant que le combat à Ypres ne s'achève, les Anglais auraient perdu 60.000 hommes, les Français 10.000 et les Allemands près de 35.000.

Mais les pertes à Ypres n'étaient rien, comparées à celles qui allaient bientôt suivre à Verdun, en France. Le matin d'une brillante journée enneigée, le 21 février 1916, à 7h15, après s'être préparée pendant huit mois, toute l'artillerie allemande commença à tomber sur les forteresses et les tranchées françaises encer-clant la ville. Et, pendant les dix heures qui suivirent, sous une pluie constante d'obus, les Français dans les tranchées–blottis et priant–attendirent la fin de l'attaque.

Avant midi de cette première journée aucune construction habitable ne restait debout dans aucun des neuf villages voisinant Verdun; la chaleur de centaines de milliers, voire de millions d'explosions d'artillerie avait fait fondre la couche de neige qui, à peine quelques heures plus tôt, recouvrait les champs et les toits de la campagne. On n'y voyait plus qu'un monde de boue, glacial, criblé de cratères creusés par les bombes.

C'est alors qu'on arrive à la partie la plus terrifiante du siège. Juste avant le coucher du soleil, alors que le tir de barrage avait finalement cessé, les Allemands ont commencé leur avance. Et, dans les tranchées autour de Verdun, tandis qu'une marée de regel atteignait les genoux des Français, les défenseurs de Verdun qui avaient été épargnés par les explosions ou les éclats d'obus se préparaient à défendre leur ville. Le paysage qui les séparait de leurs agresseurs était déchiqueté. Les explosions d'artillerie avaient dénudé des forêts entières, ne laissant que des piquets d'arbres fumants, la végétation elle-même ayant été pulvérisée. À la place des arbres, il n'y avait plus maintenant que les traces des explosions et une nappe de boue.

Mais les Allemands avaient encore une autre horreur en réserve. Pour s'assurer que le champ de bataille était complètement débarrassé d'obstacles pendant ce crépuscule d'une violence sans égal, ils *décidèrent de raser les dernières broussailles qui restaient et d'abattre les derniers arbres en étrennant leur invention la plus récente: le lance-flammes.*

Tandis que ces cracheurs de feu commençaient à avancer, les combattants français calèrent leurs fusils entre les mottes de terre devant leurs tranchées et commencèrent à se défendre. Très vite, les Français s'étaient aperçus que s'ils tiraient sur le réservoir à carburant que chaque lanceur de flammes portait sur son dos, il explosait. Des centaines de fantassins allemands furent ainsi immolés; les autres continuaient d'avancer. Au bout d'une heure, les Allemands avaient atteint les tranchées et les deux armées commencèrent à se mutiler les uns les autres avec les moyens du bord: couteaux et poings, pierres et crosses de fusils.

Dans les collines surplombant Verdun, ce type de combat n'a pas cessé, chaque jour, pendant dix mois; puis il piétina, pendant 18 mois de plus. Et tout cela pour contester une ligne de bataille qui n'avait avancé et reculé que de quelques kilomètres à la fin de la guerre. Quand le siège de Verdun fut finalement levé, plus de 1.000.000 de soldats avaient été engloutis par le combat. Qui plus est, ce sont peut-être les statistiques de guerre les plus horribles de l'histoire, seulement 290.000 corps ont été récupérés, dont 160.000 seulement identifiés. Les autres ont simplement été enlevés du champ de bataille en morceaux.

Au bout du compte, la majorité des millions d'hommes tombés sur le champ de bataille de Verdun, soit plus de 710.000 soldats (nombre suffisant pour peupler une grande ville)—ont été simplement portés disparus, avalés par les explosions et la boue. Le nouveau monde mécanisé du XXe siècle les avait détruits complètement. Dans la comptabilité impitoyable de la guerre moderne, le groupe dans sa totalité fut simplement réduit à néant.

Ces sortes de tragédies peuvent marquer des paysages à jamais.

Pour Jane Alden Stevens, le défi résidait dans son désir de rendre les pertes de la Grande Guerre à travers des images en regard oblique. Elle y a réussi d'une manière incroyable.

Personne ne peut regarder l'image de l'eau ruisselant le long des marches de marbre du Mémorial naval de Chatham en Grande-Bretagne (Planche No 26) sans imaginer, ne serait-ce qu'un seul instant, que ce ruissellement d'eau trouble est du sang. Dans les photos de paysages, il est impossible de ne pas remarquer que, près de 90 ans après la fin de la guerre, la terre est toujours abîmée et défigurée par les cratères creusés par les bombes. Examinez la petite zone détruite par l'artillerie, près de la Colline 62 à Ypres (seuls deux monticules de terre la séparent de la zone où le gaz toxique fut utilisé pour la première fois durant la guerre)(Planche No 14). Les arbres ont repoussé pour couvrir le sol de leur ombre, mais le témoignage des bombardements de l'horrible printemps de l'année 1915 est indubitable. De vieilles tranchées mènent à une fortification tout aussi ancienne et l'éclat de l'eau boueuse au fond de la tranchée évoque un mois d'avril froid et pluvieux, où règnent les gaz asphyxiants et les explosions de l'artillerie. On peut presque sentir les balles fendre l'air au-dessus des tranchées.

Dans la photo de Stevens prise du haut de Fort Douaumont (Planche No 1), cet endroit tragique, dont les murs de ciment d'un gris terne sont tombés entre les mains des Allemands cinq jours après le début du siège, devenu un tombeau pour 679 Allemands morts dans un seul accident de munitions survenu à l'intérieur–domine un enchevêtrement de barbelés emboutis les uns aux autres datant de 1916. Le nid de fils d'acier rongés par la rouille semble dire: oui, on se souvient de ces pertes de vie, cet endroit est vénéré. Mais, d'une manière obsédante, les hommes modernes sont absents de la photo.

«Une des choses que j'ai voulu accomplir dans ce projet» dit Stevens, «c'était d'explorer la persistance de la mémoire humaine. Nous rappelons-nous activement les pertes des guerres datant d'époques bien plus anciennes que la nôtre? De quelle manière l'importance des mémoriaux que nous construisons à la suite d'une guerre persiste-t-elle avec le temps? Et comment la terre elle-même nous rappelle-t-elle la violence de notre passé?»

Y a-t-il des paysages hantés sur la terre? Et comment! Il suffit de tourner la page.

DONOVAN WEBSTER

AUTEUR, AFTERMATH: THE REMNANTS OF WAR

*I have seen wonders
today - what horrors
did you see? Rest in Pea*

"I have seen wonders today—what horrors did you see? Rest in peace."

(QUOTATION PHOTOGRAPHED FROM VISITORS BOOK AT A WAR MEMORIAL IN FRANCE)

ARTIST'S ESSAY   ESSAY DER KÜNSTLERIN   *ESSAI DE L'ARTISTE*

*W*HILE ON A TRIP TO FRANCE, I found myself one day standing in a small town square. My eye wandered to an obelisk in the center of the square. On it were written the years 1914–18, and under each year were listed the names of villagers who had fallen.

As I further studied this monument, I saw that many names were listed under 1914, even more for 1915 and '16, but far fewer for 1917, and hardly any for 1918. "Why the falloff in numbers?" I asked myself. And then it struck me. There were no more men or boys that this village could send to war. They had already gone.

The casualty figures from the First World War are appalling. Of the men mobilized by the three major Western Front powers, 76.3% of the French troops were either killed, injured, taken prisoner, or suffered the unknown fate of the missing. Germany lost 64.9% of its armed forces, and the British Empire 35.8%. In total, French casualties, including the dead, wounded, and missing, numbered more than 6,000,000 (17% of its total male population), Germany more than 7,000,000 (15.4%), and the British Empire just over 3,000,000 (12.5%).[1] It is no wonder that the term "Lost Generation" was often used to refer to these soldiers. Whether the men were lost physically or psychologically, huge numbers of civilians were directly affected by their fate. The result was a world that was forever changed.

The unprecedented number of wartime casualties introduced the concept that when a country loses a huge portion of its population in war, it has a need to publicly acknowledge, honor, and defend the sacrifice. As a result, thousands of national, local, and private memorials were built in Western Front countries. These places were, and continue to be, sites of remembrance, along with the hundreds of military cemeteries that were built along the front itself. The vast majority of these are kept in immaculate condition. The military cemeteries all have books in which visitors can write down their observations about the experience of being there and their thoughts about the war.

After deciding to undertake this project, I initially focused on man-made sites such as monuments, cemeteries, and statuary, which are the most outwardly visible manifestations of grief and memorialization of the war. I also photographed mementos left behind by pilgrims to these places. As the project progressed, however, I became increasingly aware of the role that the landscape itself plays

---

[1] Susanne Everett and Brigadier Peter Young, *The Two World Wars* (Greenwich, CT: Bison Books Corp., 1984), pp. 248, 249.

as a repository of memory. Nothing is more telling than the continued existence of a "red zone" in France, vast tracts of land where entry is forbidden because of the sheer number of unexploded shells still lodged in the ground. It was not unusual to find bits of shrapnel beside artifacts such as horseshoes in farmers' fields; and seeing shells lying by the side of the road waiting for pickup by the French Demining Agency was a daily occurrence in certain regions.

In France and Belgium a number of shell-pocked landscapes remain as they were when the war ended. Some have become open-air memorial parks, while others are being used for everyday purposes, such as grazing horses. Many shell craters have been converted into farm ponds where geese and ducks now swim. A sense of lingering evil and desolation infuses the air of some of these places, as if the ground itself cannot shake off the burden of the lives lost upon it. The land on which the First World War was fought retains the memory of it still, and will for generations to come.

Whether it is a landscape formed by the violence of man and left to remind us of the cataclysm that produced it, or a physical structure built by man to honor those lost to that violence, the human impulse to memorialize lost loved ones is profound. The photographs in this book are the result of the journey I began that day in the square and act as both a reminder of the ongoing cost of historical events and a mirror to the human heart.

DEFINING EXPERIENCES

When working on any creative project, an artist invariably has experiences that become defining moments. Sometimes these are a result of serendipity—simply being in the right place at the right time. Other times they are a result of having carefully observed the subject and its environment for an extended period. The following experiences are among the most significant I had while shooting "Tears of Stone."

Shell Hole

Nine villages in the hills above Verdun, France, suffered complete destruction during a ten-month battle in 1916. One of them, the village of Fleury-devant-Douaumont, had more than 400 inhabitants and changed hands 16 times over the course of a few weeks at the height of the conflict. Nothing remained standing.

I drove up to the site and parked the car. Set back from the road and running parallel to it was a tall barbed-wire fence bearing warning signs due to the unexploded shells still in the ground beyond it. I realized that this was part of the cordon rouge, or "red zone," the tracts of land in France that have yet to be fully demined. On the other side of the road, the terrain looked like a bizarre moonscape. There was no even ground anywhere, except for some paths that had been carved out between the hillocks. I followed one of these paths, which follow the course of the former village streets, down a hill, then turned left onto another. Three-foot-high pedestals with trilingual signs appeared, marking the locations where the baker, farmer, butcher, road repairer, and other village artisans and merchants used to live. A few piles of moss-covered brick rubble and the pedestals were the only evidence that the village had ever existed in this distorted landscape.

Although the land of the village proper was successfully demined, the chemicals from the shells had so devastated the soil that Fleury, along with eight other villages nearby, was not allowed to be rebuilt. Any crops grown there would have been unfit for human consumption. Therefore, all of these villages' former inhabitants were permanently displaced, never to return home. Seeing the water-filled shell hole into which the contaminated village spring of Fleury flows filled me with sorrow. Although the cause of the water's toxicity lies more than 85 years in the past, it is yet another reminder of the long-term impact the war had on the land, and on the people who had lived there.

Lone Surviving Tree

Of the 3,153 men of the South African Brigade who fought in the 1916 Battle of Delville Wood in France, 75% became casualties.[2] The forest itself was obliterated, with only a single hornbeam surviving. The woods have since been replanted, and a large memorial and museum have been built on site to honor the South African efforts in both world wars. Behind the museum and on either side of it are overgrown trenches from the battle that visitors can wander through.

To the left of the museum is the hornbeam, standing alone from the other trees that have grown where visitors leave artifacts, perhaps because it is the only living link to the men who died there. Most of the mementos are small crosses with red poppies in the center, left behind by citizens of the

[2] Nigel Cave, *Delville Wood: Somme* (Barnsely, South Yorkshire, England: Leo Cooper, 1999), p. 27.

British Commonwealth, and with short messages scrawled on them. The crosses have been left either at the base of the tree or in the fissures of its trunk where it has healed around its wounds. The bark has been worn smooth in spots where many hands have touched it over the years. It is clear how sacred the tree is and how honored it is for its resiliency. Its continued existence serves as a connection across the years to those who died there.

On the day I visited, it was very cloudy and cold. After hours of waiting in vain for the sun to come out, I decided to go ahead and photograph the tree anyway. No sooner had I put the camera into position, then a soft shaft of late-afternoon sunlight broke through the cloud cover, suddenly illuminating both the tree and the ground around it. I caught my breath, so powerful had the tree's presence become when bathed in light. I snapped the shutter as the sun disappeared, just as swiftly as it had arrived.

Wreath with Water

It had poured all morning, but the rain had just stopped when I arrived at the Chatham Naval Memorial. The sky was still deeply overcast and threatening, and the wind was blowing fiercely.

The site of the memorial is very imposing. It sits atop a high bluff overlooking Chatham, England, with a sheer cliff in front of it, empty moors to the east and south, and a small road leading up to it on a ridge from the north. The memorial itself is graceful and beautiful, with a tall obelisk rising from its center. Below the column are bronze panels containing the names of World War I naval casualties, and it is surrounded by a circular wall carrying the names of those lost at sea during World War II.

I wandered around the memorial for a while, the whole time hearing snatches of music that would come and go with each gust. In walking around to the front of the obelisk, I discovered a wreath that had blown over lying at its base. I propped it back up as a gesture of respect and walked down toward the lip of the cliff to a good vantage point. When I turned around to photograph, I saw that the water that had apparently collected in the wreath from the overnight rain had begun to drain out of it and flow toward me.

It was a totally unexpected sight, almost shocking in how much the water looked like blood in all but color. The flute music seemed lower now and more constant despite the strong wind. I stood there frozen for a moment, too many thoughts swirling around in my head to easily sort out. In the few minutes it took me to photograph the scene, the wind had dried the water. It was almost as if it had never existed, although the musical notes sporadically kept drifting in.

As I left, I immediately saw the source of the music: a young woman (probably 17 or 18) who was slowly walking through the moors that abut the memorial. It appeared as though she was walking home from school—she wore a small backpack, and her head was slightly bent over a recorder. I recognized the song as a Celtic lament, the notes of which drifted in and out at the will of the wind. The coalescence of the wreath, the water, and the music was unforgettable, a perfect summation of sorrow, pain, and remembrance.

Fairy Ring

While in the Somme region of France, I decided one day to take a short cut via a dirt road that led up a very large hill through some farmers' fields. After reaching the top, I rechecked my map and discovered that two small British military cemeteries were located nearby within hiking distance of each other. On a whim, I stopped and walked to the nearest one, Redan Ridge No. 3. Other than the cemeteries and a village in the distance, nothing but fields was in view. The silence was profound.

I approached the cemetery and entered. It was quite small, with just over 50 graves. After wandering around a bit and not finding much to photograph, I left, intending to walk to the next one. But something tugged at me about this place. I felt I was leaving prematurely but couldn't explain why. I turned around and went back in, but still nothing spoke to me. Frustrated and dissatisfied, I left the cemetery once again, this time taking a slightly different path. Almost at once, my eye was caught by something on the ground. The reason I had been called there became instantly clear.

A mature fairy ring, comprised of mushrooms growing out of the low grass surrounding the cemetery, lay in front of me. It is unusual to see a fairy ring, much less one at its peak, for they appear only under certain climatic conditions. A day or two later this ring would have vanished, mushrooms being somewhat ephemeral, and I never would have known it had been there.

Ancient European folklore ascribed magical powers to these rings, and it did not seem accidental to find one in this location. It appeared to be guarding the cemetery, which is located in what used to be the German front-line trenches in this part of the Somme region. I never made it to my original destination that afternoon, preferring to spend time in a place in which the works of nature were seamlessly woven together with the works of humankind.

Langemarck Letter

A high stone wall surrounds the Langemarck German Cemetery, near the Belgian city of Ypres. Entry is gained by passing through a stone blockhouse, which is extremely dim inside, even on a sunny day. Its oak-paneled walls have been carved with the names of the missing. Light streams in from the open door opposite the entryway, and the opening serves as a frame for four shadowy figures standing sentinel on the opposite side of the cemetery. (I later discovered these were statues of grieving soldiers.) After passing through the doorway, I encountered a mass grave containing the remains of 25,000 unidentified German soldiers immediately in front me. It was surrounded by bronze panels containing more names of the missing and was planted over with low shrubs. Lying at the front of the grave was a letter that had been laminated to protect it from the weather, with a single red rose fastened to it. The letter, written in German, had 24 signatures on it and read as follows:

> *We, the 10th grade class from the Friesenschule in Leer, East Friesland, Germany, have come to this sad place to better understand the terrible event of the 1914–1918 war.*
>
> *It is difficult for our generation to understand from books and texts the unimaginable suffering and despair of the millions of soldiers who fell in the war. Therefore... we are visiting certain important sites of the First World War, including this one.*
>
> *We are visiting this site of memory in the hope that:*
>
> > *—mankind will never again take part in such a terrible event, which completely ignored every aspect of human dignity over the course of 4 years;*
> >
> > *—the memory of this senseless war with its tears, desperation, and the suffering of those left behind will never be extinguished.*
>
> *With this in mind, we appeal to all people in all countries to learn to live together in peace, and therefore*
>
> *NO MORE WAR!*

I was deeply impressed that a class of teenagers had traveled so far from home in order to learn more about an event that lay so far in the past. I was equally impressed with the care and passion they had obviously invested in the writing of this letter. But given the nature of human beings as has been proven over millennia, it is not likely that their wish for an end to all war will find fulfillment. I gazed down at the grave before me, feeling more powerfully than ever the importance of remembrance and being grateful that I was there that day.

JANE ALDEN STEVENS

*W*ÄHREND EINES AUFENTHALTS IN FRANKREICH fand ich mich eines Tages auf einem kleinen Dorfplatz wieder. Mein Auge wanderte zu dem Denkmal in der Mitte des Platzes. Auf dem Obelisken standen die Jahre 1914–18 geschrieben, unter jedem Jahr fanden sich die Namen der gefallenen Dorfbewohner.

Als ich das Monument weiter betrachtete, sah ich, daß unter dem Jahr 1914 viele Namen aufgeführt waren, mehr noch unter den Jahren 1915 und 1916, aber weitaus weniger für 1917 und kaum welche für 1918. „Warum ist die Zahl so gesunken?" fragte ich mich lange. Plötzlich wußte ich. Es gab keine Männer oder Jungen mehr, die dieses Dorf in den Krieg schicken konnte. Sie waren alle schon fort.

Die Todesraten im Ersten Weltkrieg sind erschreckend. Von den Männern, welche die drei großen westlichen Frontmächte mobilisiert hatten, wurden 76,3% der französischen Truppen entweder getötet, verletzt, gefangen genommen oder sie erlitten das Schicksal des „Unbekannten Soldaten". Deutschland verlor 64,9% seiner Armee und das Britische Weltreich 35,8%. Insgesamt betrug die Anzahl der französischen Gefallenen einschließlich der Toten, Verwundeten und Vermißten mehr als 6.000.000 (17% der männlichen Bevölkerung), auf deutscher Seite mehr als 7.000.000 (15,4%) und für das Britische Empire knapp über 3.000.000 (12,5%).[1] Es wundert nicht, daß der Begriff der „verlorenen Generation" oft im Zusammenhang mit diesen Soldaten benutzt wurde. Ob die Männer physisch oder psychisch verloren gingen, eine gewaltige Anzahl von Zivilisten war von diesem Schicksal direkt betroffen. Das Ergebnis war eine für alle Zeit veränderte Welt.

Die noch nie zuvor dagewesene Zahl von Kriegsgefallenen führte dazu, daß sich viele Staaten veranlaßt sahen, ihre Toten öffentlich zu ehren und um sie zu trauern. Folglich wurden tausende nationaler, lokaler und privater Gedenkstätten in den Ländern der Westfront gebaut. Diese Orte waren und sind immer noch Schauplätze des Erinnerns; gemeinsam mit den hunderten an Militärfriedhöfen, die entlang der Front selbst gebaut wurden. Die große Mehrzahl dieser Stätten wird in makellosem Zustand gehalten. Die Militärfriedhöfe verfügen allesamt über Bücher, in die Besucher ihre Beobachtungen, ihre eigenen Erfahrung oder allgemeine Gedanken über den Krieg niederschreiben können.

Nachdem ich mich entschlossen hatte, dieses Projekt zu realisieren, konzentrierte ich mich zunächst auf die von Menschenhand geschaffenen Schauplätze wie Monumente, Friedhöfe und Statuen,

---

[1] Susanne Everett und Brigadier Peter Young, *The Two World Wars* (Greenwich, CT: Bison Books Corp., 1984), S. 248f.

wo die Manifestation des Kummers und die Erinnerung an den Krieg am deutlichsten sichtbar werden. Ich sah auch Fotografien von Mahnzeichen, welche von Pilgern an diesen Stätten zurückgelassen wurden.

Im Verlauf des Projektes wurde mir jedoch immer mehr die Rolle der Landschaft selbst als Erinnerungsspeicher bewußt. Nichts ist bezeichnender als das Fortbestehen einer „Roten Zone" in Frankreich: riesige Landstriche, deren Betreten aufgrund der hohen Anzahl an Blindgängern, die sich immer noch im Boden befinden, verboten ist. Es war nicht ungewöhnlich, neben Artefakten wie Hufeisen oder Granatsplittern, Bomben auf den Feldern zu finden. Bauern hatten Markierungen am Straßenrand angebracht, um den französischen Sprengmittelräumkommandos die Lage der gefährlichen Blindgänger anzuzeigen.

In Frankreich und Belgien blieb eine Anzahl mit Bombentrichtern übersäter Landschaften so, wie sie bei Kriegsende waren. Aus einigen wurden Gedächtnisparks, andere werden für alltägliche Zwecke wie Weideland für grasende Pferde verwendet. Aus vielen Bombentrichtern wurden Wasserlöcher für die Landwirtschaft, in denen jetzt Gänse und Enten schwimmen. Die Luft einiger dieser Orte ist mit einer beklemmenden Ahnung belastet, als ob der Boden nicht die Last der auf ihm verlorenen Leben abschütteln könnte. Das Land, auf dem der Erste Weltkrieg ausgetragen wurde, hält die Erinnerung für viele Generationen wach.

Ganz gleich, ob es eine Landschaft ist, die durch die Gewalt der Menschen geschändet wurde und nun daliegt, um uns an die Katastrophe zu erinnern, oder ob es eine physische Struktur ist, die von den Menschen geschaffen wurde, um diejenigen zu ehren, die durch diese Gewalt verloren gingen. Der menschliche Impuls, sich an die verlorenen Lieben zu erinnern, ist grundlegend. Die Bilder in diesem Buch sind das Ergebnis einer Reise, die ich an dem Tag antrat, an dem ich auf dem Dorfplatz stand. Sie dienen der Erinnerung an die historischen Ereignisse wie auch als Spiegel für das Herz der Menschen.

SCHLÜSSELERLEBNISSE

Bei der Arbeit an einem kreativen Projekt macht ein Künstler stets Erfahrungen, die zu Schlüsselerlebnissen werden. Manchmal entstehen diese nur durch einen glücklichen Zufall–einfach dadurch, daß man zur rechten Zeit am rechten Ort ist. Manchmal aber sind sie das Ergebnis sorgfältiger Beobachtung des Gegenstands und seiner Umgebung für einen gewißen Zeitraum. Die folgenden

Erfahrungen zählen zu den bedeutendsten Erfahrungen, die ich machte, während ich die Bilder für „Tränen aus Stein" aufnahm.

Bombenkrater

Neun Dörfer in den Hügeln über Verdun, Frankreich, wurden während der zehn Monate andauernden Schlacht im Jahre 1916 vollständig zerstört. Eines von ihnen, das Dorf Fleury-devant-Douaumont, hatte mehr als 400 Einwohner und war das letzte Hindernis, das den deutschen Vormarsch in die Stadt Verdun blockierte. Im Laufe weniger Wochen, auf dem Höhepunkt des Konflikts, wechselte es 16 mal den Besitzer. Nichts blieb übrig.

Ich fuhr an den Schauplatz und parkte den Wagen. Parallel zur Straße verlief ein hoher Stacheldrahtzaun mit Warnschildern vor Blindgängern, die noch immer in der Erde dahinter liegen. Mir wurde klar, daß dies ein Teil des Cordon Rouge oder der „Roten Zone" war; die Gebiete in Frankreich, die noch immer darauf warten, vollständig entmint zu werden. Auf der anderen Seite der Straße sah die Gegend wie eine bizarre Mondlandschaft aus. Es gab nirgends ebenen Grund, mit Ausnahme einiger Pfade, die zwischen den Hügeln eingeschnitten waren. Ich folgte einem dieser Pfade, die dem Verlauf der ehemaligen Dorfstraßen entsprachen. Der Pfad führte den Hügel hinunter und bog dann links ab. Niedrige Sockel mit dreisprachigen Schilder tauchten auf und markierten die Orte, wo der Bäcker, der Bauer, der Metzger, der Straßenarbeiter sowie andere Handwerker und Händler des Dorfes gelebt hatten. Ein paar moosbewachsene Backsteinhügel und die Sockel waren der einzige Hinweis darauf, daß es das Dorf in dieser entstellten Landschaft jemals gegeben hat.

Wenn auch der Boden des Dorfes selbst erfolgreich entmint wurde, haben die Chemikalien aus den Bomben das Erdreich doch derart verwüstet, daß Fleury, zusammen mit anderen Dörfern in der Nähe, nicht wieder aufgebaut werden durfte. Alle landwirtschaftlichen Erzeugnisse, die dort angebaut würden, wären nicht zum Verzehr durch den Menschen geeignet. Daher wurden alle ehemaligen Einwohner dieser Dörfer dauerhaft umgesiedelt und durften nicht wieder heimkehren. Kummer ergriff mich, als ich die mit Wasser gefüllten Bombentrichter sah, in welche die verseuchte Dorfquelle von Fleury floß. Obwohl die Ursache der Verseuchung mehr als 85 Jahre zurückliegt, ist sie eine weitere Erinnerung an die langfristigen Auswirkungen des Krieges auf Land und Menschen.

Der einzige überlebende Baum

Von den 3.153 Männern der Südafrikanischen Brigade, die 1916 in der Schlacht im Wald von Delville kämpften, fielen 75%.[2] Der Wald selbst wurde ausradiert, nur eine einzige Buche überlebte. Der Wald ist in der Zwischenzeit wieder aufgeforstet. Eine große Gedenkstätte mit Museum ehrt den südafrikanischen Beitrag zu beiden Weltkriegen. Hinter dem Museum und zu seinen beiden Seiten sind überwucherte Schützengräben aus der Schlacht verblieben, welche die Besucher durchwandern können.

Auf der linken Seite des Museums steht die Buche. Sie steht abseits von den anderen Bäumen, die seit dem Krieg auf dem Schlachtfeld gewachsen sind. Das Schild in der Nähe erzählt ihre Geschichte. Der Baum ist der einzige Ort im Park, an dem Besucher Gegenstände zurücklassen, vielleicht weil er die einzige lebendige Verbindung zu den Männern ist, die hier gestorben sind. Viele der Andenken sind kleine Kreuze mit roten Mohnblumen in der Mitte, die von Bürgern des Britischen Commonwealth zurückgelassen wurden und auf denen kurze Nachrichten gekritzelt sind. Die Kreuze werden entweder am Fuße des Baumes zurückgelassen oder in den mittlerweile vernarbten Wunden des Stammes. Die Rinde ist glatt gerieben von den vielen Händen, die sie im Lauf der vielen Jahre berührten. Es ist unverkennbar, wie heilig der Baum ist und wie sehr er für diese Widerstandskraft verehrt wird. Sein fortwährendes Bestehen dient als Verbindung über all die Jahre hinweg zu denen, die dort gestorben sind.

An dem Tag, an dem ich dort zu Besuch war, war es sehr wolkig und kalt. Nachdem ich stundenlang vergeblich auf die Sonne gewartet hatte, brachte ich meine Kamera dennoch in Position. Es verschlug mir den Atem als ein weicher Strahl spätnachmittäglichen Sonnenlichts durch die Wolkendecke brach und lediglich den Baum und den Boden um ihn herum erhellte. Ich drückte auf den Auslöser in dem Moment, in dem die Sonne wieder verschwand, genauso flink, wie sie erschienen war.

Der weinende Kranz

Es hatte den ganzen Morgen stark geregnet. Der Himmel war immer noch bedeckt, und ein drohender Wind blies unablässig, als ich die Marinegedenkstätte von Chatham erreichte.

[2] Nigel Cave, *Delville Wood: Somme* (Barnsely, South Yorkshire, England: Leo Cooper, 1999), S. 27.

Der Ort ist sehr imposant. Die Gedenkstätte liegt auf einem hohen Steilufer, das Chatham, England, überragt, mit einer scharfen Klippe davor, Mooren links und rechts sowie einer schmalen Straße, die auf dem Bergrücken von Norden zu ihr hinaufführt. In der Mitte des anmutigen Ortes erhebt sich ein großer Obelisk, auf dessen Sockel die Namen der im Ersten Weltkrieg gefallenen Soldaten aufgeführt sind.

Ich spazierte eine Zeit um die Gedenkstätte und hörte immer wieder Musikfetzen, die mir der böige Wind zutrug. Als ich an der Vorderseite des Obelisken vorüberging, entdeckte ich einen umgewehten Kranz. Als Zeichen der Achtung richtete ich ihn wieder auf und lief hinunter zur Klippe, um einen guten Blickwinkel zu suchen. Als ich mich umdrehte, um zu fotografieren, sah ich, daß das Wasser, das sich vom nächtlichen Regen offenbar im Kranz gesammelt hatte, in einem kleinen Rinnsal auf mich zufloß.

Es war ein vollkommen unerwarteter Anblick. Beinahe schockierend wie das Wasser an das vergossene Blut erinnerte. Die Flötenmusik schien jetzt trotz des starken Windes lauter und beständiger zu sein. Bewegungslos blieb ich für einen Moment stehen. Zu viele Gedanken wirbelten durch meinen Kopf, als daß ich sie leicht hätte sortieren können. Innerhalb der wenigen Minuten, die ich brauchte, um die Gedenkstätte zu fotografieren, hatte der Wind das Wasser getrocknet. Es war beinahe so, als ob es nie existiert hätte.

Als ich ging, sah ich sofort die Quelle der Musik: eine junge Frau (wahrscheinlich 17 oder 18), die langsam durch die Moore wanderte. Es schien, als ob sie auf dem Heimweg von der Schule war–sie trug einen kleinen Rucksack, und ihr Kopf war leicht über einen Recorder geneigt. Ich erkannte das Lied als eine keltische Klage, die Töne drifteten nach dem Willen des Windes hinein und hinaus. Das Zusammentreffen des Kranzes, des Wassers und der Musik war unvergeßlich, eine beeindruckende Verschmelzung von Kummer und Leid der Erinnerung.

Der Hexenring

Als ich im französischen Departement Somme war, beschloß ich, einen kurzen Abstecher über einen Feldweg zu machen. Dieser führte auf einen sehr großen Hügel. Auf dem Gipfel angekommen entdeckte ich beim Betrachten der Landkarte, daß sich ganz in der Nähe zwei britische Militärfriedhöfe befanden. Sie waren so nahe beieinander, daß sie zu Fuß erreichbar waren. Kurz entschlossen hielt ich an und lief zu dem näher gelegenen, Redan Ridge No. 3. Außer den Friedhöfen und dem Dorf in der Ferne waren nur Felder zu sehen. Die Stille war allumfassend.

Mit etwas mehr als 50 Gräbern war der Friedhof sehr klein. Nachdem ich ein wenig herumgegangen war und nicht viel gefunden hatte, das ich hätte fotografieren können, ging ich wieder und wollte zum nächsten Friedhof gehen. Aber irgendetwas an diesem Ort berührte mich. Ich hatte den Eindruck, voreilig weggegangen zu sein, aber ich konnte nicht erklären warum. Ich machte kehrt und ging zurück. Frustriert und unzufrieden verließ ich den Friedhof noch einmal und nahm diesmal einen etwas anderen Weg. Plötzlich fiel mein Blick auf etwas am Boden. Augenblicklich wurde klar, dies war der Grund, warum ich zurückgekehrt war.

Ein voll entwickelter Hexenring: Pilze, die auf dem niedrigen Gras vor dem Friedhof wuchsen. Ein solcher Hexenring ist eine Rarität, noch ungewöhnlicher ist es, einen in vollem Wachstum zu sehen, denn sie treten nur unter bestimmten Klimabedingungen auf. Einen Tag später wäre der Ring verschwunden gewesen. Die Pilze sind kurzlebig, ich hätte niemals von ihrer Anwesenheit erfahren.

Im Altertum schrieb man diesen Ringen magische Kräfte zu, und es schien kein Zufall zu sein, daß ich einen an diesem Ort vorfand. Er schien den Friedhof zu beschützen, ehemals waren dies die deutschen Schützengräben an der Kampffront in jenem Teil von Somme. An diesem Nachmittag habe ich es nicht bis zu meinem ursprünglich geplanten Ziel geschafft, denn ich zog es vor, die Zeit an einem Ort zu verbringen, an dem das Werk der Natur nahtlos mit dem Werk der Menschheit verwoben war.

Der Langemarck-Brief

Eine hohe Steinmauer umgibt den deutschen Soldatenfriedhof Langemarck in der Nähe der belgischen Stadt Ypern. Der Eingang führt durch ein Blockhaus aus Stein, welches selbst an sonnigen Tagen sehr dunkel ist. In die mit Eichenholz getäfelten Wände sind die Namen der Vermißten eingraviert. Licht fällt durch die offene Türe gegenüber dem Eingangsflur, und die Öffnung dient als Rahmen für vier schattenhafte Figuren, die auf der gegenüberliegenden Seite des Friedhofs Wache stehen. (Ich entdeckte später, daß diese Statuen trauernde Soldaten waren.) Nachdem ich durch den Flur gegangen war, traf ich auf ein Massengrab direkt vor mir mit den Überresten von 25.000 nicht identifizierten deutschen Soldaten. Es war umgeben von Bronzetafeln, mit weiteren Namen der Vermißten und überwachsen von niedrigen Büschen. Vor dem Grab lag ein Brief, eingeschweißt in Plastikfolie zum Schutz vor der

Witterung und geschmückt mit einer einzigen rote Rose. Der deutschsprachige Brief trug 24 Unterschriften und lautete wie folgt:

> *Um das schreckliche Geschehen der Jahre von 1914 bis 1918 besser*
> *nachvollziehen zu können, sind wir, die Klasse 10a der Friesenschule*
> *aus Leer Ostfriesland, an diesen traurigen Ort gekommen.*
>
> *Das unvorstellbare Leid und die Verzweiflung über die Millionen*
> *gefallenen Soldaten sind für unsere Generation aus Büchern und Texten*
> *nur sehr schwer nachzuempfinden, deshalb haben wir (dieses Jahr)*
> *einige Stätten des ersten Weltkriegs–darunter auch diese aufgesucht.*
>
> *In der Hoffnung:*
>
>> *–daß Menschen sich nie wieder an solchen schrecklichen*
>> *Vorgängen, die unter Mißachtung jeglicher Menschenwürde*
>> *über vier Jahre hier stattgefunden haben, beteiligen,*
>>
>> *–und daß die Erinnerung an diesen sinnlosen Krieg mit seinen*
>> *Tränen, seiner Verzweiflung und dem Leid der Zurückgebliebenen*
>> *niemals verlöschen wird, besuchen wir diese Gedenkstätte.*
>
> *In diesem Sinne appellieren wir an alle Menschen in allen Staaten:*
> *Laßt uns nicht gegen–sondern miteinander leben, deshalb*
>
> ### *NIE WIEDER KRIEG!*

Ich war zutiefst beeindruckt, daß eine Schulklasse mit Teenagern so weit gereist war, um mehr über ein so lange zurückliegendes Ereignis zu erfahren. Auch die Sorgfalt und Leidenschaft, mit der sie offenbar diesen Brief geschrieben hatten, war beeindruckend. Aber angesichts der menschlichen Natur, wie sie sich über Jahrtausende erwiesen hat, ist es unwahrscheinlich, daß ihr Wunsch nach einem Ende aller Kriege erfüllt wird. Ich betrachtete das vor mir liegende Grab und fühlte die Bedeutung der Erinnerung stärker als jemals zuvor. Ich war dankbar, an diesem Tag dort gewesen zu sein.

JANE ALDEN STEVENS

*L*ORS D'UN VOYAGE EN FRANCE, *je me suis retrouvée un jour sur la place d'une petite ville. Mon regard errant s'arrêta sur l'obélisque qui se dressait au centre de la place et sur lequel on avait inscrit les années 1914–18; au-dessous de chaque année inscrite, il y avait la liste des noms des villageois qui étaient tombés durant la guerre.*

Au fur et à mesure que j'examinais ce monument, je me suis aperçue que beaucoup de noms étaient inscrits sous l'année 1914, qu'il y en avait encore plus pour 1915 et 1916, mais beaucoup moins pour 1917 et à peine quelques-uns uns pour 1918. «Pourquoi une telle décroissance numérique?» me demandai-je. Et puis la réponse m'est venue à l'esprit: Il ne restait plus d'hommes ni de garçons dans ce village susceptibles d'être envoyés à la guerre. Ils étaient déjà partis.

Le nombre des morts et des blessés durant la Première Guerre mondiale, c'est à dire la Grande Guerre, est horrifiant. Parmi les hommes mobilisés par les trois puissances du Front Occidental, 76,3% des soldats français furent tués, blessés, faits prisonniers ou subirent le destin inconnu des soldats portés disparus. L'Allemagne avait perdu 64,9% de son armée et l'Empire britannique 35,8%. Au total, le nombre de victimes en France, y compris les morts, les blessés et les disparus, dépassait 6 millions (17% de sa population totale masculine); l'Allemagne en comptait plus de 7 millions (15,4%) et l'Empire britannique un peu plus de 3 millions (12,5%).[1] Il n'est pas étonnant que le terme «génération perdue» ait été souvent employé pour désigner ces soldats. Perdus physiquement ou psychologiquement, un très grand nombre de civils ont été directement affectés par leur destin. Le résultat était un monde qui avait changé pour toujours.

Le nombre sans précédent des victimes de cette guerre a introduit le concept qui fait que lorsqu'un pays perd une partie énorme de sa population au combat, il doit reconnaître, honorer et défendre publiquement leur sacrifice. En conséquence, des milliers de monuments commémoratifs nationaux, locaux et privés ont été construits dans les pays du Front Occidental. Ces endroits étaient et continuent à être des lieux de souvenir, tout comme les centaines de cimetières militaires construits le long du front même. En grande majorité, ces derniers sont maintenus dans un état immaculé. Les cimetières militaires sont tous dotés de registres où les visiteurs peuvent noter leurs réflexions sur l'expérience de leur visite, ainsi que leurs pensées au sujet de la guerre.

---

[1] *Susanne Everett et Brigadier Peter Young,* The Two World Wars *(Greenwich, CT: Bison Books Corp., 1984), p. 248, 249.*

Au début, je me suis concentrée sur certains sites édifiés par l'homme, tels que les monuments, les cimetières et les statues, qui sont les manifestations extérieures les plus visibles du chagrin et de l'immortalisation des souvenirs de guerre. J'ai également photographié des souvenirs laissés par des pèlerins qui avaient visité ces endroits.

Cependant, à mesure que le projet avançait, je suis devenue de plus en plus consciente du rôle que le paysage lui-même joue comme recueil de mémoire. Rien n'est plus expressif que l'existence continue de cette «zone rouge» en France, où l'accès à de vastes étendues de terres est interdit en raison du nombre incroyable d'obus non explosés, toujours enfouis dans le sol. Il n'était pas rare de trouver des éclats d'obus à côté d'artefacts comme des fers à cheval dans les champs; l'observation d'obus posés au bord de la route attendant leur ramassage par l'organisme de déminage français était un fait journalier dans certaines régions.

En France et en Belgique, des paysages criblés d'obus sont restés tels quels depuis la fin de la guerre. Certains sont devenus des parcs commémoratifs en plein air, tandis que d'autres sont employés pour les besoins courants, servant par exemple de pâturages aux chevaux. Beaucoup de cratères d'obus ont été convertis en petits étangs fermiers où oies et canards s'ébattent à présent. Dans certains de ces endroits, un sentiment persistant et funeste de désolation insuffle l'air, comme si la terre elle-même ne pouvait pas se débarrasser du fardeau des vies perdues. La terre qui a vu les batailles de la Grande Guerre en garde le souvenir et le conservera pour des générations à venir.

Qu'il s'agisse d'un paysage produit par la violence humaine et laissé ainsi pour nous rappeler ce cataclysme qui l'a produit ou d'une structure matérielle édifiée par l'homme pour honorer ceux qui ont disparu dans cette violence, la réaction humaine de commémorer des êtres chers disparus est profonde. Les photographies de ce livre sont le résultat du voyage que j'ai commencé ce jour-là, sur cette place; d'une part, elles témoignent du poids continu des événements historiques, et d'autre part, elles servent de miroir au cœur humain.

EXPÉRIENCES DÉTERMINANTES

Quel que soit le projet créateur, un artiste connaît invariablement des expériences qui deviennent des moments déterminants. Celles-ci sont quelquefois le résultat d'un heureux hasard—en étant simplement au bon endroit au moment propice. D'autres fois elles sont le résultat d'une observation soigneuse et prolongée du sujet et de son environnement. Les expériences suivantes sont parmi les plus importantes que j'ai vécues pendant que j'effectuais les prises de vue de «Tears of Stone» («Larmes de pierre»).

Trou d'obus

En 1916, neuf villages situés dans les collines surplombant Verdun, en France, ont été entièrement détruits pendant une bataille de dix mois. L'un d'entre eux, le village de Fleury-devant-Douaumont, avait une population de plus de 400 habitants, c'était le dernier obstacle bloquant l'avance allemande vers la ville de Verdun. Situé en plein cœur du conflit, le village a changé de mains seize fois en quelques semaines de combat. Rien n'en est resté.

J'ai roulé jusqu'au site et garé la voiture. Un peu en retrait de la route et disposée parallèlement à cette dernière, il y avait une haute clôture en fil barbelé portant des panneaux signalant la présence d'obus non explosés se trouvant toujours dans la terre au-delà du barbelé. Je me suis rendu compte que ce site faisait partie du Cordon Rouge ou de «la zone rouge», les terres en France pas encore entièrement déminées. De l'autre côté de la route, le paysage était lunaire. Il n'y avait pas une trace de terrain plat, à part quelques chemins qui avaient été aménagés entre les monticules. J'ai emprunté l'un des chemins qui suivent le cours des anciennes rues du village, descendant une colline, puis j'ai tourné à gauche pour en prendre un autre. Des piédestaux d'un mètre de haut portant des panneaux trilingues apparurent, marquant les endroits où habitaient le boulanger, le fermier, le boucher, le cantonnier et d'autres artisans et marchands du village. Les piédestaux et quelques décombres de briques recouverts de mousse étaient les seuls indices prouvant l'existence du village dans ce paysage déformé.

Bien que les terrains du village même aient été déminés avec succès, les produits chimiques provenant des obus avaient dévasté le sol à tel point que la reconstruction de Fleury et de huit autres villages situés dans le voisinage n'a pas été autorisée. Toute récolte provenant de ces terres aurait été impropre à la consommation. En conséquence, les anciens habitants de tous ces villages ont été déplacés de façon permanente et ne sont jamais retournés chez eux. Rien que le fait de voir rempli d'eau le cratère d'obus dans lequel coulait la source contaminée du village de Fleury, m'a remplie de tristesse. Bien que la cause de la toxicité de l'eau remonte à plus de 85 ans, elle reste un souvenir vivace de l'impact à long terme que la guerre a produit sur les terres et les gens qui y ont vécu.

L'arbre solitaire qui avait survécu

Parmi les 3.153 hommes de la brigade sud-africaine ayant participé en 1916 à la bataille du Bois de Delville en France, il y a eu 75% de victimes.[2] La forêt elle-même a été rayée de la carte; seul un charme a survécu. Les bois ont été replantés depuis et un grand mémorial et un musée ont été construits sur le site pour honorer les efforts des Sud-Africains durant les deux guerres mondiales. Derrière le musée et de chaque côté, les visiteurs peuvent se promener dans les tranchées de la bataille, envahies par les broussailles.

À gauche du musée, il y a le charme, cet arbre qui se dresse seul, isolé des autres arbres qui ont poussé sur le champ de bataille depuis la guerre. Un panneau à côté raconte son histoire. L'arbre est l'unique endroit du parc où les visiteurs laissent des objets, peut-être parce qu'il est le seul lien vivant avec les hommes qui sont morts là. La plupart des souvenirs consistent en de petites croix avec des coquelicots rouges au centre, laissées par des citoyens du Commonwealth britannique, avec de courts messages gribouillés dessus. Les croix ont été soit déposées au pied de l'arbre, soit insérées dans les fissures du tronc, là où il a guéri de ses blessures. L'écorce est parsemée de taches lisses, aux endroits où de nombreuses mains l'ont touchée au cours des années. On comprend combien cet arbre est sacré et combien il est honoré pour sa résistance. Son existence même perpétue le lien, à travers toutes ces années, avec ceux qui sont morts sur ces lieux.

Le jour de ma visite, le ciel était très nuageux et il faisait froid. Après avoir attendu, en vain, pendant des heures, l'apparition du soleil, j'ai décidé de photographier l'arbre quand même. À peine avais-je mis en place l'appareil photographique qu'un faible rai de soleil perça la couche de nuages, illuminant subitement l'arbre et le terrain qui l'entoure. J'ai retenu mon souffle, frappée par la présence si puissante de l'arbre baigné de lumière. À peine avais-je pris la photo que le soleil disparut aussi vite qu'il était apparu.

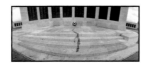

Couronne imbibée d'eau

Il avait plu à verse toute la matinée, mais la pluie venait de s'arrêter quand je suis arrivée au mémorial naval de Chatham. Le ciel était toujours profondément couvert et menaçant et le vent soufflait avec acharnement.

Le site du mémorial est très imposant. Il se trouve au sommet d'un promontoire abrupt surplombant

[2] *Nigel Cave*, Delville Wood: Somme *(Barnsely, South Yorkshire, England: Leo Cooper, 1999), p. 27.*

Chatham, en Angleterre, avec une falaise à pic en face, une lande déserte à l'est et au sud et une petite route en corniche qui y mène par le nord. Le mémorial lui-même est beau et gracieux, avec un haut obélisque se dressant au milieu. Au-dessous de la colonne, des panneaux de bronze portent les noms de soldats de la marine, victimes de la Première Guerre mondiale; elle est entourée d'un mur circulaire portant les noms des disparus en mer pendant la Deuxième Guerre mondiale.

J'errai autour du mémorial pendant quelque temps, ne cessant d'entendre des notes de musique qui allaient et venaient avec chaque rafale. En contournant l'obélisque, je découvris, gisant à sa base, une couronne renversée. Dans un geste de respect, je l'ai remise en place et je suis descendue vers le bord de la falaise pour avoir un bon point d'observation. Quand je me suis retournée pour prendre des photos, je me suis aperçue que l'eau accumulée dans la couronne par la pluie de la nuit précédente commençait à s'écouler vers moi.

C'était une vision totalement inattendue, presque choquante, du fait que l'eau ressemblait à du sang, excepté la couleur. La musique de la flûte semblait résonner plus fort à présent et d'une manière plus constante, malgré la force du vent. Je restai figée sur place pendant un moment; trop de pensées tourbillonnaient dans ma tête pour pouvoir facilement les démêler. Pendant les quelques minutes passées à photographier la scène, le vent avait asséché l'eau. C'était presque comme si cela n'avait jamais existé, même si les notes de musique continuaient à se faire entendre sporadiquement.

Au moment où je partais, je découvris immédiatement la source de cette musique: une jeune fille (âgée probablement de 17 à 18 ans) marchait lentement à travers la lande aboutissant au mémorial. Elle semblait rentrer chez elle, venant de l'école; elle portait un petit sac à dos et sa tête était légèrement courbée sur une flûte à bec. Je reconnus la chanson d'une complainte celte, dont les notes se laissaient aller au gré du vent. La coalescence de la couronne, de l'eau et de la musique était inoubliable, représentant en union parfaite à la fois la tristesse, la douleur et le souvenir.

Rond de sorcière

Quand j'étais dans la région de la Somme, en France, j'ai décidé un jour de prendre un raccourci à travers champs par un chemin de terre battue qui menait en haut d'une très grande colline. Après avoir atteint le sommet, j'ai vérifié de nouveau ma carte et découvert que deux petits cimetières militaires britanniques se trouvaient tout près, à quelques minutes de marche l'un de l'autre. Je me suis arrêtée, je ne sais pas pourquoi, et je me suis dirigée vers le plus proche, Redan Ridge No 3. À part les cimetières et un village au loin, on ne voyait que des champs. Il y régnait un profond silence.

Je me suis approchée du cimetière et j'y suis entrée. Il était assez petit et comportait à peine plus de 50 tombes. Après avoir fait une petite promenade aux alentours et n'ayant rien trouvé à photographier, je décidai d'aller en direction du cimetière suivant. Mais quelque chose me retenait dans cet endroit. Je pressentais que je partais trop vite, mais je ne pouvais en expliquer la raison. J'ai fait demi-tour et j'y suis retournée, mais rien n'était venu encore m'éclairer l'esprit. Frustrée et mécontente, j'ai quitté le cimetière à nouveau, empruntant cette fois un chemin légèrement différent. Presque aussitôt, mon regard fut attiré par quelque chose sur le sol. La raison pour laquelle j'y avais été appelée devint immédiatement très claire.

Un rond de sorcière mûr, composé de champignons croissant au milieu d'herbes basses qui entouraient le cimetière, s'étalait devant moi. Il est peu commun de voir un rond de sorcière, surtout au moment de sa maturation, car ils n'apparaissent que dans des conditions climatiques particulières. Un jour ou deux plus tard, ce rond de sorcière aurait disparu, les champignons étant quelque peu éphémères, et je n'aurais jamais su qu'il avait été là.

L'ancien folklore européen attribuait des pouvoirs magiques à ces ronds de sorcière et il ne semblait pas accidentel d'en trouver un dans cet endroit. Il semblait garder le cimetière qui se trouve sur l'emplacement des tranchées du front allemand dans cette partie de la région de la Somme. Je ne suis jamais parvenue à mon lieu de destination d'origine cet après-midi-là, préférant consacrer du temps à un lieu où les travaux de la nature s'entrelaçaient harmonieusement avec ceux de l'humanité.

La lettre de Langemarck

Un haut mur en pierre entoure le cimetière allemand de Langemarck, près de la ville belge d'Ypres. On y pénètre en passant à travers un blockhaus dont l'intérieur est extrêmement sombre, même les jours ensoleillés. Sur ses murs lambrissés de chêne, on a sculpté les noms des disparus. La lumière entre à flots par la porte face à l'entrée et l'ouverture sert de cadre à quatre personnages mystérieux qui montent la garde de l'autre côté du cimetière. (J'ai découvert plus tard qu'il s'agissait de statues de soldats pleurant leurs morts.) Après avoir franchi le seuil, je vis juste devant moi une fosse commune contenant les restes de 25.000 soldats allemands non identifiés. Elle était entourée de panneaux de bronze portant les noms d'autres disparus, et recouverte de petits arbustes.

Exposée devant la fosse commune, il y avait une lettre, laminée pour la protéger contre les intempéries; une seule rose rouge y était attachée. La lettre, écrite en allemand, portait 24 signatures; on pouvait y lire ce qui suit:

> *Nous, élèves de la classe de 3ème du collège Friesenschule, à Leer, Friesland de l'Est, en Allemagne, sommes venus visiter ce triste endroit pour mieux comprendre les terribles événements de la guerre 1914–1918.*
>
> *Il est difficile pour notre génération de comprendre par la lecture de livres et de textes la souffrance inimaginable et le désespoir des millions de soldats qui sont tombés à la guerre. Pour cette raison... nous visitons certains sites importants liés à la Première Guerre mondiale, y compris celui-ci.*
>
> *Nous visitons ce site de mémoire dans l'espoir que:*
>
> > *–L'humanité ne participera plus jamais à un aussi terrible événement, qui a complètement ignoré tous les aspects de la dignité humaine durant 4 ans;*
> >
> > *–le souvenir de cette guerre insensée avec ses larmes, son désespoir et la souffrance de ceux qui y sont restés, ne soit jamais effacé.*
>
> *Avec ce souvenir à l'esprit, nous lançons un appel à tous les peuples, dans tous les pays, d'apprendre à vivre ensemble dans la paix et par conséquent*
>
> ### *PLUS JAMAIS DE GUERRE!*

Je fus profondément impressionnée qu'une classe d'adolescents ait fait un voyage si loin de chez eux pour mieux comprendre un événement si éloigné dans le passé. Je fus tout aussi impressionnée par le soin et la passion qu'ils avaient manifestement démontrés en rédigeant cette lettre. Mais, étant donné la nature humaine, comme il a été prouvé durant des millénaires, il est peu probable que leur vœu de voir l'homme mettre fin à toute guerre se réalise. J'ai jeté mon regard sur la tombe devant moi, ressentant plus fermement que jamais l'importance du souvenir, et heureuse de m'y être trouvée ce jour là.

JANE ALDEN STEVENS

*There but for the grace
of God. Go I*

"There but for the grace of God. Go I."

(QUOTATION PHOTOGRAPHED FROM VISITORS BOOK AT A WAR MEMORIAL IN FRANCE)

PLATES   ABBILDUNGEN   *PLANCHES*

[PLATE 1]

FORT DOUAUMONT, FRANCE

Fort Douaumont, Frankreich

Fort Douaumont, France

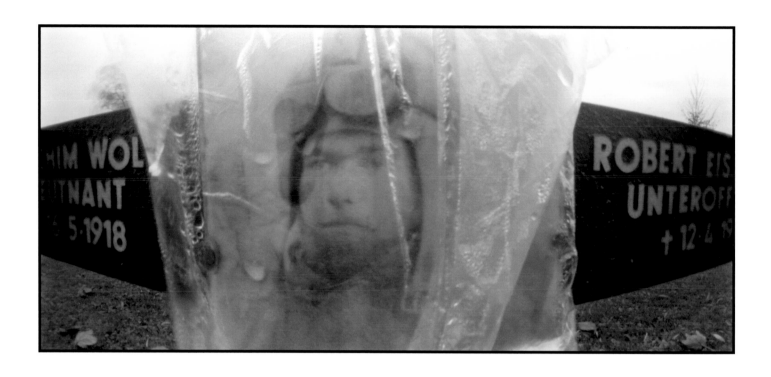

[PLATE 2]

MEMENTO, VERMANDOVILLERS GERMAN
MILITARY CEMETERY, FRANCE

Andenken, Deutscher Soldatenfriedhof
Vermandovillers, Frankreich

Mémento, Cimetière militaire
allemand de Vermandovillers, France

[PLATE 3]

VERMANDOVILLERS GERMAN
MILITARY CEMETERY, FRANCE

Deutscher Soldatenfriedhof
Vermandovillers, Frankreich

*Cimetière militaire allemand
de Vermandovillers, France*

[P L A T E 4]

CHEPPY GERMAN MILITARY
CEMETERY, FRANCE

Deutscher Soldatenfriedhof
Cheppy, Frankreich

*Cimetière militaire allemand
de Cheppy, France*

[PLATE 5]

VLADSLO GERMAN
MILITARY CEMETERY, BELGIUM

Deutscher Soldatenfriedhof
Vladslo, Belgien

*Cimetière militaire allemand
de Vladslo, Belgique*

[PLATE 6]

EPITAPH, BROOKWOOD MILITARY
CEMETERY (BRITISH), ENGLAND

Grabinschrift, Britischer Militärfriedhof
Brookwood, England

Épitaphe, cimetière militaire
anglais de Brookwood, Angleterre

[PLATE 7]

BREITENBACH GERMAN
MILITARY CEMETERY, FRANCE

Deutscher Soldatenfriedhof
Breitenbach, Frankreich

Cimetière militaire allemand
de Breitenbach, France

[PLATE 8]

CHEVAUX-DE-FRISE,
BUTTE DE VAUQUOIS, FRANCE

Chevaux-de-frise,
Butte de Vauquois, Frankreich

Chevaux-de-frise,
Butte de Vauquois, France

[PLATE 9]

WARMERIVILLE GERMAN
MILITARY CEMETERY, FRANCE

Deutscher Soldatenfriedhof
Warmeriville, Frankreich

*Cimetière militaire allemand
de Warmeriville, France*

[PLATE 10]

LA BELLE ALLIANCE MILITARY
CEMETERY (BRITISH), BELGIUM

Britischer Militärfriedhof
La Belle Alliance, Belgien

Cimetière militaire anglais
de La Belle Alliance, Belgique

[PLATE 11]

SITE OF FORMER VILLAGE OF
FLEURY-DEVANT-DOUAUMONT, FRANCE

Ort des ehemaligen Dorfes
Fleury-devant-Douaumont, Frankreich

Site de l'ancien village de
Fleury-devant-Douaumont, France

[PLATE 12]

ROMAGNE-SOUS-MONTFAUCON
GERMAN MILITARY CEMETERY, FRANCE

Deutscher Soldatenfriedhof
Romagne-sous-Montfaucon, Frankreich

Cimetière militaire allemand de
Romagne-sous-Montfaucon, France

[PLATE 13]

MUNICIPAL WAR MEMORIAL,
MONTFAUCON, FRANCE

Kriegerdenkmal der Gemeinde
Montfaucon, Frankreich

*Monument aux morts municipal
de Montfaucon, France*

[PLATE 14]

TRENCH, HILL 62,
YPRES, BELGIUM

Schützengraben, Hügel 62,
Ypern, Belgien

Tranchée, Colline 62,
Ypres, Belgique

[PLATE 15]

REDAN RIDGE NO. 3 MILITARY
CEMETERY (BRITISH), FRANCE

Britischer Militärfriedhof
Redan Ridge No. 3, Frankreich

Cimetière militaire anglais
Redan Ridge No. 3, France

[PLATE 16]

SHELL HOLE NEAR
VERDUN, FRANCE

Bombenkrater in der Nähe
von Verdun, Frankreich

*Cratère d'obus près
de Verdun, France*

[PLATE 17]

MUNICIPAL WAR MEMORIAL,
YPRES, BELGIUM

Kriegerdenkmal der Gemeinde
Ypern, Belgien

Monument aux morts municipal
d'Ypres, Belgique

[PLATE 18]

HEADSTONES, BROOKWOOD MILITARY
CEMETERY (BRITISH), ENGLAND

Grabsteine, Britischer Militärfriedhof
Brookwood, England

*Pierres tombales, Cimetière militaire
anglais de Brookwood, Angleterre*

[PLATE 19]

BEDFORD HOUSE MILITARY
CEMETERY (BRITISH), BELGIUM

Britischer Militärfriedhof
Bedford House, Belgien

Cimetière militaire anglais
de Bedford House, Belgique

I am sure that it would hav
so many people still care enong

"I am sure that it would have given them some comfort to k

(QUOTATION PHOTOGRAPHED FROM VISI

en them some comfort to know that

visit after so long a time ...

o many people still care enough to visit after so long a time."

T A MILITARY CEMETERY IN FRANCE)

[PLATE 20]

MENIN GATE (BRITISH MEMORIAL
TO THE MISSING), BELGIUM

Das Menin Tor, Britische Gedenkstätte
für die Vermißten, Belgien

*Monument aux disparus anglais
de Menin Gate, Belgique*

[PLATE 21]

VOORMEZEELE ENCLOSURES
NO. 1&2 (BRITISH), BELGIUM

Britischer Militärfriedhof Voormezeele
Enclosures No. 1&2, Belgien

Cimetière militaire anglais de Voormezeele
Enclosures No. 1&2, Belgique

[PLATE 22]

ACHIET-LE-PETIT GERMAN
MILITARY CEMETERY, FRANCE

Deutscher Soldatenfriedhof
Achiet-le-Petit, Frankreich

*Cimetière militaire allemand
d'Achiet-le-Petit, France*

[PLATE 23]

MEMORIAL,
BUTTE DE VAUQUOIS, FRANCE

Kriegerdenkmal,
Butte de Vauquois, Frankreich

Mémorial de la
Butte de Vauquois, France

[PLATE 24]

DARTMOOR MILITARY
CEMETERY (BRITISH), FRANCE

Britischer Militärfriedhof
Dartmoor, Frankreich

*Cimetière militaire anglais
de Dartmoor, France*

[PLATE 25]

AUBERIVE GERMAN
MILITARY CEMETERY, FRANCE

Deutscher Soldatenfriedhof
Auberive, Frankreich

Cimetière militaire allemand
d'Auberive, France

[PLATE 26]

CHATHAM NAVAL
MEMORIAL, ENGLAND

Marinegedenkstätte
Chatham, England

*Mémorial naval
de Chatham, Angleterre*

[PLATE 27]

ST.-CHARLES-DE-POTYZE
FRENCH MILITARY CEMETERY, BELGIUM

Französischer Militärfriedhof
St.-Charles-de-Potyze, Belgien

*Cimetière militaire français
de St.-Charles-de-Potyze, France*

[PLATE 28]

FRENCH CIVILIAN AND GERMAN MILITARY
CEMETERIES, ACHIET-LE-PETIT, FRANCE

Französischer Zivilfriedhof und
deutscher Soldatenfriedhof, Achiet-le-Petit, Frankreich

*Cimetière civil français et cimetière
militaire allemand d'Achiet-le-Petit, France*

[PLATE 29]

LANGEMARCK GERMAN
MILITARY CEMETERY, BELGIUM

Deutscher Soldatenfriedhof
Langemarck, Belgien

*Cimetière militaire allemand
de Langemarck, Belgique*

[PLATE 30]

FIGURES, LANGEMARCK GERMAN
MILITARY CEMETERY, BELGIUM

Statuen, Deutscher Soldatenfriedhof
Langemarck, Belgien

*Statues, cimetière militaire allemand
de Langemarck, Belgique*

[PLATE 31]

AMMERSCHWIR-TROIS-EPIS
GERMAN MILITARY CEMETERY, FRANCE

Deutscher Soldatenfriedhof
Ammerschwir-Trois-Epis, Frankreich

*Cimetière militaire allemand
d'Ammerschwir-Trois-Epis, France*

[PLATE 32]

VILLERS-CARBONNEL
FRENCH MILITARY CEMETERY, FRANCE

Französischer Militärfriedhof
Villers-Carbonnel, Frankreich

Cimetière militaire
français de Villers-Carbonnel, France

[PLATE 33]

MUNICIPAL WAR MEMORIAL,
CHÂTEAU-THIERRY, FRANCE

Kriegerdenkmal der Gemeinde
Château-Thierry, Frankreich

*Monument aux morts municipal
de Château-Thierry, France*

[PLATE 34]

VILLERS-COTTERÊTS
FRENCH MILITARY CEMETERY, FRANCE

Französischer Militärfriedhof
Villers-Cotterêts, Frankreich

*Cimetière militaire francais
de Villers-Cotterêts, France*

[PLATE 35]

MENEN GERMAN MILITARY
CEMETERY, BELGIUM

Deutscher Soldatenfriedhof
Menen, Belgien

Cimetière militaire allemand
de Menen, Belgique

[PLATE 36]

LONE SURVIVING TREE FROM THE
BATTLE OF DELVILLE WOOD, FRANCE

Der einzige überlebende Baum der
Schlacht von Delville Wood, Frankreich

*Seul arbre subsistant de la
bataille de Delville Wood, France*

[PLATE 37]

GERMAN MILITARY CEMETERY,
BAD ORB, GERMANY

Deutscher Soldatenfriedhof
Bad Orb, Deutschland

*Cimetière militaire allemand
de Bad Orb, Allemagne*

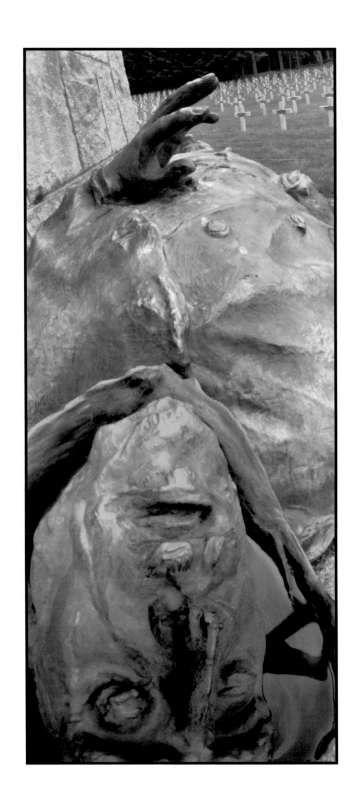

LE WETTSTEIN, FRENCH MILITARY CEMETERY, FRANCE

Französischer Militärfriedhof Le Wettstein, Frankreich | *Le Wettstein, Cimetière militaire français, France*

[PLATE 39]

BERKS CEMETERY EXTENSION (BRITISH), BELGIUM

Britischer Militärfriedhof Berks Cemetery Extension, Belgien | *Cimetière militaire anglais de Berks Cemetery Extension, Belgique*

[PLATE 40]

RANCOURT MILITARY
CEMETERY (BRITISH), FRANCE

Britischer Militärfriedhof
Rancourt, Frankreich

*Cimetière militaire
anglais de Rancourt, France*

PLATE LIST   LISTE *der* ABBILDUNGEN   *LISTE des PLANCHES*

THE NEGATIVE SIZE OF ALL PINHOLE PHOTOGRAPHS IS 2 1/8" X 4 5/8", WHILE
THE NEGATIVE SIZE OF ALL LENS-BASED PICTURES IS 2" X 5".

Die Negativgröße der Lochkamera-Fotografien beträgt 5.5cm x 11.8cm, während
die Blendenkamera-Negative 5cm x 12cm groß sind.

*La taille des négatifs de toutes les photos au sténopé est de 5,5cm x 11,8cm, les négatifs
de toutes les photos à lentilles conventionnelles sont de 5cm x 12cm.*

[PLATE 10]

LA BELLE ALLIANCE MILITARY CEMETERY (BRITISH), BELGIUM, PINHOLE IMAGE, 2001 | Britischer Militärfriedhof La Belle Alliance, Belgien, Lochkamera-Foto, 2001 | *Cimetière militaire anglais de La Belle Alliance, Belgique, Photo par Sténopé, 2001*

[PLATE 11]

SITE OF FORMER VILLAGE OF FLEURY-DEVANT-DOUAUMONT, FRANCE, PINHOLE IMAGE, 2001 | Ort des ehemaligen Dorfes Fleury-devant-Douaumont, Frankreich, Lochkamera-Foto, 2001 | *Site de l'ancien village de Fleury-devant-Douaumont, France, Photo par Sténopé, 2001*

[PLATE 12]

ROMAGNE-SOUS-MONTFAUCON GERMAN MILITARY CEMETERY, FRANCE, PINHOLE IMAGE, 2001 | Deutscher Soldatenfriedhof Romagne-sous-Montfaucon, Frankreich, Lochkamera-Foto, 2001 | *Cimetière militaire allemand de Romagne-sous-Montfaucon, France, Photo par Sténopé, 2001*

[PLATE 13]

MUNICIPAL WAR MEMORIAL, MONTFAUCON, FRANCE, PINHOLE IMAGE, 2003 | Kriegerdenkmal der Gemeinde Montfaucon, Frankreich, Lochkamera-Foto, 2003 | *Monument aux morts municipal de Montfaucon, France, Photo par Sténopé, 2003*

[PLATE 14]

TRENCH, HILL 62, YPRES, BELGIUM, PINHOLE IMAGE, 2001 | Schützengraben, Hügel 62, Ypern, Belgien, Lochkamera-Foto, 2001 | *Tranchée, Colline 62, Ypres, Belgique, Photo par Sténopé, 2001*

[PLATE 15]

REDAN RIDGE NO. 3 MILITARY CEMETERY (BRITISH), FRANCE, LENS IMAGE, 2001 | Britischer Militärfriedhof Redan Ridge No. 3, Frankreich, Blendenkamera-Foto, 2001 | *Cimetière militaire anglais Redan Ridge No. 3, France, Photo avec Objectif, 2001*

[PLATE 16]

SHELL HOLE NEAR VERDUN, FRANCE, LENS IMAGE, 2001 | Bombenkrater in der Nähe von Verdun, Frankreich, Blendenkamera-Foto, 2001 | *Cratère d'obus près de Verdun, France, Photo avec Objectif, 2001*

[PLATE 17]

MUNICIPAL WAR MEMORIAL, YPRES, BELGIUM, PINHOLE IMAGE, 2001 | Kriegerdenkmal der Gemeinde Ypern, Belgien, Lochkamera-Foto, 2001 | *Monument aux morts municipal d'Ypres, Belgique, Photo par Sténopé, 2001*

[PLATE 18]

HEADSTONES, BROOKWOOD MILITARY CEMETERY (BRITISH), ENGLAND, PINHOLE IMAGE, 2002 | Grabsteine, Britischer Militärfriedhof Brookwood, England, Lochkamera-Foto, 2002 | *Pierres tombales, Cimetière militaire anglais de Brookwood, Angleterre, Photo par Sténopé, 2002*

[PLATE 19]

BEDFORD HOUSE MILITARY CEMETERY (BRITISH), BELGIUM, PINHOLE IMAGE, 2002 | Britischer Militärfriedhof Bedford House, Belgien, Lochkamera-Foto, 2002 | *Cimetière militaire anglais de Bedford House, Belgique, Photo par Sténopé, 2002*

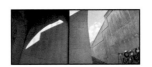

[PLATE 20]

MENIN GATE (BRITISH MEMORIAL TO THE MISSING), BELGIUM, LENS IMAGE, 2001 | Das Menin Tor, Britische Gedenkstätte für die Vermißten, Belgien, Blendenkamera-Foto, 2001 | *Monument aux disparus anglais de Menin Gate, Belgique, Photo avec Objectif, 2001*

[PLATE 21]

VOORMEZEELE ENCLOSURES NO. 1&2 (BRITISH), BELGIUM, LENS IMAGE, 2001 | Britischer Militärfriedhof Voormezeele Enclosures No. 1&2, Belgien, Blendenkamera-Foto, 2001 | *Cimetière militaire anglais de Voormezeele Enclosures No.1&2 , Belgique, Photo avec Objectif, 2001*

[PLATE 22]

ACHIET-LE-PETIT GERMAN MILITARY CEMETERY, FRANCE, PINHOLE IMAGE, 2001 | Deutscher Soldatenfriedhof Achiet-le-Petit, Frankreich, Lochkamera-Foto, 2001 | *Cimetière militaire allemand d'Achiet-le-Petit, France, Photo par Sténopé, 2001*

[PLATE 23]

MEMORIAL, BUTTE DE VAUQUOIS, FRANCE, PINHOLE IMAGE, 2002 | Kriegerdenkmal, Butte de Vauquois, Frankreich, Lochkamera-Foto, 2002 | *Mémorial de la Butte de Vauquois, France, Photo par Sténopé, 2002*

[PLATE 24]

DARTMOOR MILITARY CEMETERY (BRITISH), FRANCE, PINHOLE IMAGE, 2002 | Britischer Militärfriedhof Dartmoor, Frankreich , Lochkamera-Foto, 2002 | *Cimetière militaire anglais de Dartmoor, France, Photo par Sténopé, 2002*

[PLATE 25]

AUBERIVE GERMAN MILITARY CEMETERY, FRANCE, LENS IMAGE, 2002 | Deutscher Soldatenfriedhof Auberive, Frankreich, Blendenkamera-Foto, 2002 | *Cimetière militaire allemand d'Auberive, France, Photo avec Objectif, 2002*

[PLATE 26]

CHATHAM NAVAL MEMORIAL, ENGLAND, LENS IMAGE, 2001 | Marinegedenkstätte Chatham, England, Blendenkamera-Foto, 2001 | *Mémorial naval de Chatham, Angleterre, Photo avec Objectif, 2001*

[PLATE 27]

ST.-CHARLES-DE-POTYZE FRENCH MILITARY CEMETERY, BELGIUM, PINHOLE IMAGE, 2003 | Französischer Militärfriedhof St.-Charles-de-Potyze, Belgien, Lochkamera-Foto, 2003 | *Cimetière militaire français de St.-Charles-de-Potyze, France, Photo par Sténopé, 2003*

[PLATE 28]

FRENCH CIVILIAN AND GERMAN MILITARY CEMETERIES, ACHIET-LE-PETIT, FRANCE, PINHOLE IMAGE, 2001 | Französischer Zivilfriedhof und deutscher Soldatenfriedhof, Achiet-le-Petit, Frankreich, Lochkamera-Foto, 2001 | *Cimetière civil français et cimetière militaire allemand d'Achiet-le-Petit, France, Photo par Sténopé, 2001*

[PLATE 29]

LANGEMARCK GERMAN MILITARY CEMETERY, BELGIUM, PINHOLE IMAGE, 2001 | Deutscher Soldatenfriedhof Langemarck, Belgien, Lochkamera-Foto, 2001 | *Cimetière militaire allemand de Langemarck, Belgique, Photo par Sténopé, 2001*

[PLATE 30]

FIGURES, LANGEMARCK GERMAN MILITARY CEMETERY, BELGIUM, LENS IMAGE, 2001 | Statuen, Deutscher Soldatenfriedhof Langemarck, Belgien, Blendenkamera-Foto, 2001 | *Statues, cimetière militaire allemand de Langemarck, Belgique, Photo avec Objectif, 2001*

[PLATE 31]

AMMERSCHWIR-TROIS-EPIS GERMAN MILITARY CEMETERY, FRANCE, LENS IMAGE, 2002 | Deutscher Soldatenfriedhof Ammerschwir-Trois-Epis, Frankreich, Blendenkamera-Foto, 2002 | *Cimetière militaire allemand d'Ammerschwir-Trois-Epis, France, Photo avec Objectif, 2002*

[PLATE 32]

VILLERS-CARBONNEL FRENCH MILITARY CEMETERY, FRANCE, PINHOLE IMAGE, 2001 | Französischer Militärfriedhof Villers-Carbonnel, Frankreich, Lochkamera-Foto, 2001 | *Cimetière militaire français de Villers-Carbonnel, France, Photo par Sténopé, 2001*

[PLATE 33]

MUNICIPAL WAR MEMORIAL, CHÂTEAU-THIERRY, FRANCE, PINHOLE IMAGE, 2001 | Kriegerdenkmal der Gemeinde Château-Thierry, Frankreich, Lochkamera-Foto, 2001 | *Monument aux morts municipal de Château-Thierry, France, Photo par Sténopé, 2001*

[PLATE 34]

VILLERS-COTTERÊTS FRENCH MILITARY CEMETERY, FRANCE, PINHOLE IMAGE, 2003 | Französischer Militärfriedhof Villers-Cotterêts, Frankreich, Lochkamera-Foto, 2003 | *Cimetière militaire francais de Villers-Cotterêts, France, Photo par Sténopé, 2003*

[PLATE 35]

MENEN GERMAN MILITARY CEMETERY, BELGIUM, LENS IMAGE, 2002 | Deutscher Soldatenfriedhof Menen, Belgien, Blendenkamera-Foto, 2002 | *Cimetière militaire allemand de Menen, Belgique, Photo avec Objectif, 2002*

[PLATE 36]

LONE SURVIVING TREE FROM THE BATTLE OF DELVILLE WOOD, FRANCE, LENS IMAGE, 2001 | Der einzige überlebende Baum der Schlacht von Delville Wood, Frankreich, Blendenkamera-Foto, 2001 | *Seul arbre subsistant de la bataille de Delville Wood, France, Photo avec Objectif, 2001*

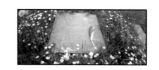

[PLATE 37]

GERMAN MILITARY CEMETERY, BAD ORB, GERMANY, PINHOLE IMAGE, 2003 |
Deutscher Soldatenfriedhof Bad Orb, Deutschland, Lochkamera-Foto, 2003 | *Cimetière militaire allemand de Bad Orb, Allemagne, Photo par Sténopé, 2003*

[PLATE 38]

LE WETTSTEIN, FRENCH MILITARY CEMETERY, FRANCE, PINHOLE IMAGE, 2001
| Französischer Militärfriedhof Le Wettstein, Frankreich, Lochkamera-Foto, 2001 |
Le Wettstein, Cimetière militaire français, France, Photo par Sténopé, 2001

[PLATE 39]

BERKS CEMETERY EXTENSION (BRITISH), BELGIUM, PINHOLE IMAGE, 2001 |
Britischer Militärfriedhof Berks Cemetery Extension, Belgien, Lochkamera-Foto, 2001 |
Cimetière militaire anglais de Berks Cemetery Extension, Belgique, Photo par Sténopé, 2001

[PLATE 40]

RANCOURT MILITARY CEMETERY (BRITISH), FRANCE, PINHOLE IMAGE, 2001 |
Britischer Militärfriedhof Rancourt, Frankreich, Lochkamera-Foto, 2001 | *Cimetière militaire anglais de Rancourt, France, Photo par Sténopé, 2001*

TECHNICAL INFORMATION   TECHNISCHE INFORMATIONEN

INFORMATIONS TECHNIQUES

UNDERTAKING *the* PROJECT

*I*NITIALLY ENVISIONED THIS EXAMINATION of World War I memorialization as a photographic exhibition. Researching the logistics of the project and writing numerous grant proposals seeking funding took a year to complete. During this period, I read many books devoted to the subject of World War I and particularly to its aftermath. Internet web sites kept me informed about local weather conditions, available daylight hours throughout the year, and specific sites that might be of interest. Because of this extensive planning period, I was ultimately able to shoot roughly 300 rolls of film at 189 various sites.

A series of camera and film tests conducted during this research phase was essential for determining which camera would yield the type of photograph I envisioned. Although all of my prior panoramic work was done on an antique Al-Vista Model 5D camera, this project required something that would be more versatile and allow me to shoot more quickly. I ultimately chose two medium format panoramic cameras, a Pinoramic 120 made by Kurt Mottweiler, and a Noblex Pro 6/150 U.

The Pinoramic 120 camera has an aperture of f/200, with a 60mm effective focal length and a 120° field of view. It yields six exposures per roll of 120 film and has a bulb-actuated pneumatic shutter. This camera allowed me to get extremely close to my subjects, while the Noblex made photographs with exquisite detail. Both of these cameras were convenient to use in the field, and the size of the medium format negatives yielded superior image resolution.

When the preliminary research was done and funding from the Ohio Arts Council, the English-Speaking Union, and the University of Cincinnati was secured, the shooting phase of the project commenced, and took almost two years to complete. I made a total of five trips to Europe, including Belgium, Germany, England, and France, with a stay of 10 to 14 days per trip. After each visit, I returned to the United States to process, print, and evaluate the results.

The limited amount of time for shooting during each trip presented a unique set of challenges. Since I did not have the luxury of staying and photographing in any given location for a prolonged period of time, every minute of each visit counted. I would arrive with a chart that outlined the time of day when sunrise, midday, sunset, and dusk occurred for the region I was to be in. In summer, I could shoot for 13 to 14 hours a day, while in winter only 8 hours of daylight were available.

Since most locations were outdoors, anticipating inclement weather was a must, regardless of the time of year I was there. Fingerless fleece gloves provided the necessary flexibility for using the cameras, and an oversized pair of snow gaiters protected my knees and shins while kneeling on wet ground. In addition, my raingear was big enough to accommodate the layers of clothing needed when shooting in winter.

The wind blew almost constantly, regardless of season or location. Since the Pinoramic 120 camera utilized long exposure times, which required absolute camera stillness, I used a lightweight but very stable tripod whose legs would not vibrate with the wind. Another useful tool was a fanny-pack style camera bag. Its design was ideal because it could be swung out of the way to rest on my back while I knelt, squatted, or lay down to photograph epitaphs or mementos close to the ground.

TEARS *of* STONE, *the* EXHIBITION

Bringing the photographs into exhibition form required careful planning. The project was shot with black-and-white film materials and digitally printed on watercolor paper. After being edited from contact prints, the negatives of the chosen images were drum scanned and retouched in PhotoShop®. The exhibition prints were made on Epson® printers with Piezography™ BW software and Quad Black inks, on Wells River (also called William Turner) paper.

Photo No. 1

The resulting exhibition, an example of which is shown above *(Photo No. 1),* is a conceptual installation that allows viewers to participate in the process of remembrance. A strip of molding is mounted below the photographs and runs continuously around the gallery walls. Scores of reproductions of pages from the cemeteries' visitors books are placed on pedestals throughout the gallery.

Photo No. 2

Viewers are asked to write down their thoughts or observations on the reverse side of these pictures and place them at any location along the molding *(Photo No. 2)*. Regardless of which side is facing out, writing is visible, and the exhibition itself takes on the character of a memorial.

REALISIERUNG *des* PROJEKTS

*U*RSPRÜNGLICH HATTE ICH DIE UNTERSUCHUNG DER GEDENKSTÄTTEN des Ersten Weltkrieges als Photoausstellung geplant. Ich habe ein Jahr gebraucht, um die Logistik dieses Projekts zu realisieren und um zahlreiche Bittschreiben für die finanzielle Unterstützung zu verschicken. In dieser Zeit las ich viele Bücher über den Ersten Weltkrieg, insbesondere über seine Nachwirkungen. Über das Internet habe ich mich über das örtliche Wetter, die zu erwartenden Tageslichtzeiten während des ganzen Jahres und über Schauplätze informiert, die von besonderem Interesse sein könnten. Durch diese große Planungszeit benötigte ich schließlich rund 300 Filme an 189 verschiedenen Schauplätzen.

Während der Vorbereitungsphase war eine Reihe von Kamera- und Filmtests erforderlich, um zu entscheiden, mit welcher Kameras ich die Bilder machen könnte, die mir vorschwebten. Alle meine vorherigen Panoramaarbeiten habe ich mit einer antiken Al-Vista-Kamera Modell 5D gemacht, aber dieses Projekt verlangte etwas vielseitigeres, was mir erlauben würde, Bilder in schnellerer Abfolge zu machen. Schließlich wählte ich zwei Panoramakameras im Mittelformat, eine von Kurt Mottweiler gebaute Pinoramic 120 und eine Noblex Pro 6/150 U.

Die Pinoramic 120 hat eine Blendenöffnung von f/200 mit 60mm effektivem Fokus und einem Öffnungswinkel von 120°. Sie liefert sechs Bilder pro Rolle 120er Film und hat einen pneumatischen Verschluß mit Fernbedienung. Diese Kamera hat es mir gestattet, sehr nahe an Objekte heranzugehen, während die Noblex vorzügliche Detailaufnahmen liefert. Beide Kameras waren vor Ort bequem zu benutzen, und die Größe der Mittelformatnegative ergab eine überragende Bildauflösung.

Als die Voruntersuchungen abgeschlossen waren und die Finanzierung durch das Ohio Arts Council, die English-Speaking Union und die Universität Cincinnati gesichert war, begann die Aufnahmephase des Projekts, deren Abschluß beinahe zwei Jahre dauerte. Ich unternahm insgesamt fünf Reisen nach Europa, nach Belgien, Deutschland, England und Frankreich, wobei jede Reise zehn bis vierzehn Tage dauerte. Nach jeder Reise kehrte ich in die Vereinigten Staaten zurück, um die Ergebnisse zu verarbeiten, um Abzüge zu machen und um sie zu bewerten.

Die begrenzte Zeit, die für die Aufnahmen zur Verfügung stand, stellte auf den Reisen eine einzigartige Herausforderung dar. Da ich nicht den Luxus hatte, für längere Zeit an den Schauplätzen zu sein und dort Bilder zu machen, zählte jede Minute eines jeden Besuchs. Bei meiner Ankunft hatte ich eine Tabelle, in der für jede Region, in der ich sein würde, verzeichnet war, wann Sonnenaufgang, Mittag, Sonnenuntergang war und wann die Dämmerung einsetzte. Im Sommer konnte ich 13 bis 14 Stunden am Tag Bilder machen, während ich im Winter nur 8 Stunden Tageslicht zur Verfügung hatte.

Da sich die meisten Schauplätze im Freien befanden, war die Vorbereitung auf rauhes Wetter ein Muß, ganz egal, zu welcher Jahreszeit ich dort war. Fingerlose Fleece-Handschuhe gaben mir die nötige Flexibilität zur Benutzung der Kameras und ein übergroßes Paar Schneegamaschen schützten meine Knie und Schienbeine, wenn ich auf nassem Boden kniete. Darüber hinaus war meine Regenkleidung weit genug, um darunter die Anzahl an Kleidungsschichten unterzubringen, die ich zum fotografieren im Winter brauchte.

Der Wind wehte beinahe immerzu–zu jeder Jahreszeit und an jedem Schauplatz. Da die Pinoramic 120 lange Belichtungszeiten brauchte, wofür wiederum die Kamera absolut still stehen mußte, benutzte ich ein leichtes, aber sehr stabiles Stativ, dessen Beine nicht mit dem Wind vibrierten. Ein weiteres nützliches Werkzeug war eine Kameratasche in der Art einer Hüfttasche. Ihre Bauart war ideal, denn ich konnte sie mir auf meinen Rücken schwingen, während ich kniete, hockte oder mich hinlegte, um Grabinschriften oder Mahnzeichen zu fotografieren, die dicht über dem Boden waren.

Um die Bilder in eine für eine Ausstellung geeignete Form zu bringen, war eine sorgfältige Planung nötig. Das Projekt wurde auf Schwarz-Weiß-Film aufgenommen, und die Abzüge wurden digital auf Aquarellpapier gemacht. Nach der Nachbearbeitung der Kontaktabzüge wurden die Negative der ausgewählten Bilder trommelgescannt und in PhotoShop® retuschiert. Die Abzüge für die Ausstellung wurden auf Epson®-Druckern mit Piezography™ BW-Software und schwarzen Tinten „Quad Black" auf Wells River-Papier (auch William Turner-Papier genannt) gemacht.

Foto Nr. 1

Die entstandene Ausstellung *(Foto Nr. 1)* ist eine konzeptuelle Installation, die es dem Betrachter gestattet am Erinnerungsprozeß teilzunehmen. Ein vertiefter Streifen unterhalb der Bilder läuft über alle Wände der Galerie durch. Reproduktionen von Auszügen aus den Besucherbüchern der Friedhöfe sind auf Ständern in der gesamten Galerie verteilt. Der Betrachter wird gebeten, seine Gedanken oder Beobachtungen auf der Rückseite dieser Bilder aufzuschreiben und sie an einen Ort seiner Wahl an dem Streifen anzubringen *(Foto Nr. 2)*. Ganz gleich, welche Seite oben ist, die Schrift ist lesbar, und die Ausstellung selbst nimmt den Charakter einer Gedenkstätte an.

Foto Nr. 2

*A*U DÉBUT, J'AVAIS ENVISAGÉ CET EXAMEN DE LA COMMÉMORATION *de la Grande Guerre dans le cadre d'une exposition de photos. Les recherches logistiques du projet et la rédaction de nombreuses propositions de subventions pour l'obtention d'un financement ont duré un an avant d'aboutir à leur réalisation. Pendant cette période, j'ai lu beaucoup de livres consacrés à la Première Guerre mondiale et en particulier à ses conséquences. Les sites de l'Internet m'ont permis d'être informée continuellement des conditions météorologiques locales, des heures de jour disponibles dans l'année et de certains sites spécifiques qui pourraient être intéressants. En raison de cette longue période de planification, je suis arrivée, en fin de compte, à consommer près de 300 rouleaux de pellicule sur 189 sites différents.*

Il m'a fallu tester une série de pellicules et d'appareils photographiques pendant cette phase de recherche, essentiel pour déterminer le meilleur type d'appareil pour produire les photographies que je voulais réaliser. Bien que tout mon travail panoramique antérieur ait été effectué avec un ancien appareil Al-ista de modèle 5D, ce projet exigeait quelque chose de plus souple et varié tout en me permettant de prendre des photos plus rapidement. Finalement, j'ai choisi deux appareils photographiques panoramiques à format moyen: un Pinoramic 120 fabriqué par Kurt Mottweiler et un Noblex Pro 6/150 U.

Le Pinoramic 120 a une ouverture de f/200, avec une distance focale de 60 mm et un angle de vision de 120°. Il permet de prendre six poses par rouleau 120 et est doté d'un déclencheur d'obturateur à distance par pompe pneumatique. Cet appareil m'a permis de m'approcher de mes sujets de très près, tandis que le Noblex m'a donné des photographies dont les détails étaient parfaits. Ces deux appareils étaient pratiques à utiliser sur le terrain et les négatifs de moyen format ont donné une résolution d'image de qualité supérieure.

Une fois la recherche préliminaire terminée et le financement du Ohio Arts Council, de English-Speaking Union et de l'Université de Cincinnati obtenus, la phase de prises de vues du projet a commencé. Elle s'est étendue sur une période de deux ans. J'ai fait au total cinq voyages en Europe, dont la Belgique, l'Allemagne, l'Angleterre et la France, avec des séjours de 10 à 14 jours par voyage. Après chaque visite, je suis retournée aux États-Unis pour le développement, le tirage et l'évaluation des résultats.

Le temps limité consacré aux prises de vues pendant chaque voyage a présenté une série de défis. Comme je n'avais pas le luxe de séjourner sur place et de photographier les endroits choisis pendant une longue période de temps, chaque minute comptait à chaque visite. J'arrivais sur place, munie d'un tableau décrivant les moments de la journée correspondant au lever du soleil, à midi, au coucher du soleil et à la tombée de la nuit pour la région visitée. En été, je pouvais prendre des photos pendant de 13 à 14 heures par jour, tandis qu'en hiver la lumière du jour ne durait que 8 heures.

Étant donné que la plupart des sites étaient en plein air, il fallait prévoir les intempéries, indépendamment de la période de l'année où je me trouvais. Des mitaines fourrées de laine polaire m'ont permis d'avoir la souplesse nécessaire pour la manipulation des appareils photographiques; une paire de guêtres polaires d'une pointure supérieure protégeait mes jambes quand je restais à genoux sur le sol humide. De plus, mon imperméable était assez grand pour accommoder les couches de vêtements nécessaires pour prendre des photos en hiver.

Le vent soufflait presque constamment, indépendamment de la saison ou de l'endroit. Comme l'appareil photo Pinoramic 120 nécessite un long temps d'exposition et demande une stabilité absolue de l'appareil, j'ai employé un trépied léger, très stable, dont les pieds ne vibraient pas sous l'action du vent. J'ai aussi utilisé un autre outil très utile: une sacoche de protection pour appareil photographique de type banane. Sa conception était idéale, car je pouvais la faire passer derrière lorsque je m'agenouillais, m'accroupissais ou m'allongeais pour photographier des épitaphes ou des souvenirs au ras du sol.

LARMES de PIERRE, L'EXPOSITION

La production de photographies en vue d'une exposition a exigé un plan minutieux. Les prises de vue du projet ont été réalisées en film noir et blanc et les photographies ont été numérisées avant d'être imprimées sur du papier pour aquarelle «watercolor». Après l'édition à partir d'épreuves-contact, les négatifs des images choisies ont été balayées par un scanner à tambour et les retouches réalisées à l'aide du logiciel

n° 1

PhotoShop®. Les épreuves de l'exposition ont été réalisées sur des imprimantes Epson®, en utilisant le logiciel Piezography™ BW et des encres noires Quad Black, sur du papier Wells River (appelé aussi William Turner).

L'exposition qui en résulte, dont on peut voir un exemple ci-dessus dans la photo n° 1, est une installation conceptuelle qui permet aux spectateurs de participer au processus commémoratif. Une bande de moulure installée sous les photographies s'étend le long des murs entourant la galerie. De nombreuses copies de pages de livres signés par les visiteurs des cimetières sont placées sur des piédestaux partout dans la galerie.

n° 2

Les visiteurs sont invités à noter leurs pensées et observations au verso de ces photos et de les placer à leur gré, le long de la moulure, comme on le voit dans la photo n° 2, ci-dessus. Ces écrits sont visibles quel que soit le coté qui se présente à la vue, ainsi l'exposition elle-même revêt un caractère commémoratif.

BIOGRAPHICAL INFORMATION   BIOGRAFISCHE INFORMATIONEN

INFORMATIONS BIOGRAPHIQUES

From "Shadowing the Gene Pool"

From "Panoramic Portraits"

From "Tears of Stone"

PRESENT

Professor of Fine Arts, *University of Cincinnati, OH*

1982

MFA in Photography, *Rochester Institute of Technology, Rochester, NY*

1974

BA in 19th-C. European Studies, *St. Lawrence University, Canton, NY*

SELECTED INDIVIDUAL EXHIBITIONS | AUSGEWÄHLTE EINZELAUSSTELLUNGEN
| SELECTION D'EXPOSITIONS PERSONNELLES

10/04

"Tears of Stone: World War I Remembered"
Johnson Museum of Art, Cornell University, Ithaca, NY

11/02

"Tears of Stone: World War I Remembered"
Blue Sky Gallery, Portland, OR

2/96

"Panoramic Portraits"
Pittsburgh Filmmaker's Gallery, Pittsburgh, PA

2/95

"Shadowing the Gene Pool"
Baldwin Photographic Gallery, MTSU, Murfreesboro, TN

12/94

"Panoramic Portraits"
A.R.C. Gallery, Chicago, IL

10/90

"New Developments"
The Center for Photography at Woodstock, NY

4/90

"New Work"
Heuser Art Center Gallery, Peoria, IL

"People in Environments"
Camera Club of New York, New York, NY

"People in Environments"
*International Photography Hall of Fame &
Museum, Oklahoma City, OK*

"Stargazing"
Southern Light Gallery, Amarillo, TX

"Dancing on a Wall"
Galerie Greisinghaus, Würzburg, West Germany

SELECTED GROUP EXHIBITIONS–JURIED *and* INVITATIONAL | AUSGEWÄHLTE

GRUPPENAUSSTELLUNGEN–BEWERTET *und* MIT EINLADUNGEN

| *SÉLECTION D'EXPOSITIONS EN GROUPE–AVEC CONCOURS et SUR INVITATION*

"Five Journeys"
Cleveland State University Art Museum, Cleveland, OH

"Heart to Heart: Women in Conversation About War"
Dahl Arts Center, Rapid City, MD

"Pan Horama 2001"
Kaukameta, Kajaani, Finland

"USA Photography"
Kharkiv Municipal Gallery, Kharkiv, Ukraine

"4th Studio of Image Technology"
Area de Convivencia do SESC Pompèia, São Paulo, Brazil

"Light Impressions Biennial Juried Show"
Spectrum Gallery, Rochester, NY

4/92
"American Photography"
Kharkiv Art Museum, Ukraine

4/91
"Selections '91"
Eye Gallery, San Francisco, CA

2/91
"Picturing Families"
Wilson Arts Center, Rochester, NY

5/89
"The Extended Image"
PhotoCentral Gallery, Hayward, CA

88–89
"Signs of Life"
Artlink Contemporary Artspace, Ft. Wayne, IN

86, 87, 89
"Illuminance"
Lubbock Fine Arts Center, Lubbock, TX

6/88
"Current Works '88"
Leedy-Voulkos Gallery, Kansas City, MO

10/87
"Images of Contemporary Women"
Lawrence Arts Center, Lawrence, KS

86–87
"Governor's Residence Art Collection"
Governor's Residence, Columbus, OH

7/86
"New Developments"
Louis K. Meisel Gallery, New York, NY

5/86
"Contemporary American Photographers"
Galerie Triangle, Washington, DC

4/84
"Rochester: An American Center of Photography"
International Museum of Photography at George Eastman House, Rochester, NY

2002

Named *"Honorary Master of Panoramic Photography"* by
the Association for Panorama Photography as an Art Form,
Tampere, Finland

1990, 2002

Ohio Arts Council Individual Artist grants

2000

English-Speaking Union Travel-Study grant

2000

Ohio Arts Council Artists Projects grant

SELECTED COLLECTIONS | AUSGEWÄHLTE SAMMLUNGEN | *SÉLECTION DE*

COLLECTIONS PERMANENTES

The Camera Club of New York
New York, NY

The Center for Photography as an Art Form
Bombay, India

The Center for Photography at Woodstock
Woodstock, NY

Cincinnati Art Museum
Cincinnati, OH

George Eastman House: International Museum of Photography and Film
Rochester, NY

Harry Ransom Humanities Research Center, University of Texas
Austin, TX

Museu da Imagem e do Som
São Paulo, Brazil

The Museum of Photography
Kharkiv, Ukraine

ACKNOWLEDGEMENTS   DANKSAGUNGEN   *REMERCIEMENTS*

I HAVE HAD MORAL, FINANCIAL, AND TECHNICAL SUPPORT FOR THIS PROJECT FROM MORE PEOPLE THAN CAN BE CITED HERE. FIRST AND FOREMOST, I THANK MY HUSBAND, GORDON BARNHART, FOR GIVING ME THE GIFT OF TIME IN ORDER TO PURSUE A PROJECT I FELT MOST PASSIONATELY ABOUT.

Mehr Menschen, als hier aufgeführt werden können, haben mich bei diesem Projekt moralisch, finanziell und technisch unterstützt. An allererster Stelle danke ich meinem Ehemann, Gordon Barnhart, daß er mir die Zeit schenkte, um dieses Projekt zu verwirklichen, dem meine ganze Leidenschaft galt.

Pour la présentation de ce projet, j'ai bénéficié du soutien moral, financier et technique de nombreuses personnes qui ne peuvent être toutes citées ici. D'abord et avant tout, je remercie mon mari, Gordon Barnhart, de m'avoir généreusement laissé le temps de poursuivre ce projet qui m'a passionnée.

TECHNICAL SUPPORT | TECHNISCHE UNTERSTÜTZUNG | *SOUTIEN TECHNIQUE*

Bill Bergh, Jon Cone, and Larry Danque, Cone Editions Press, East Topsham, VT

Adam Freedman, Meridian Printing, East Greenwich, RI

John Powers, Computer Power, Cincinnati, OH

Ann H. Stevens, East River Editorial, Rochester, NY

Jennifer Wolfe, Jennifer Wolfe Design, Rochester, NY

Susanne Barzacchini	Anne-Marie Jezequel	Thomas Palmer
Dr. Andrea Baumann-Müller	Colleen Kelley	Dr. Ulrich Pongs
Bill Buckett	Dr. Kathryn Lorenz	Wilhelm Scheer
Laurie Gilbert	Juli Lowe	Greg Southerland
Andrew Higley	Winfried Müller	Ray Walriven
	Dr. Nancy M. O'Connor	

SITE LOCATION INFORMATION | INFORMATION ZUM ORT DES GESCHEHENS | *INFORMATIONS SUR L'EMPLACEMENT DES SITES*

The Commonwealth War Graves Commission, *Great Britain*

Volksbund Deutsche Kriegsgräberfürsorge e. V., *Germany*

BACKGROUND INFORMATION | HINTERGRUNDINFORMATIONEN | *INFORMATIONS DOCUMENTAIRES*

Richard Cawood   Frederick Dann   Joan Seeman Robinson

FINANCIAL SUPPORT | FINANZIELLE UNTERSTÜTZUNG | *SOUTIEN FINANCIER*

Ohio Arts Council   University of Cincinnati   English-Speaking Union

COLOPHON

Designed by Bill Buckett and Jennifer Wolfe. Typography and production by Jennifer Wolfe Design.

Edited by Ann H. Stevens of East River Editorial. Tritone separations by Thomas Palmer, using black, two custom

grays, and a tinted varnish. *Type set in Elegant Garamond and printed in black and PMS 404.*

Printed on 115lb PhoeniXmotion Xantur paper by Meridian Printing, under the supervision of Adam Freedman.

Endleaf paper is French Paper Company's "Construction" paper in Charcoal Brown. Hardbound edition cover cloth is

Rainbow Odyssey Natural Finish in Black. *Softbound edition cover is 93lb PhoeniXmotion*

Xantur Cover. Bound by Acme Bookbinding.

BERKS CEMETERY EXTENSION (BRITISH), BELGIUM

Britischer Militärfriedhof Berks Cemetery Extension, Belgien | *Cimetière militaire anglais de Berks Cemetery Extension, Belgique*

"NEVER AGAIN"

(QUOTATION PHOTOGRAPHED FROM VISITORS BOOK AT A MILITARY CEMETERY IN FRANCE)